Reflections on Ullswater

Trans-Pennine Publishing

The CUMBRIA HERITAGE series is published by

Trans Pennine Publishing Ltd.
PO Box 10
Appleby-in-Westmorland
Cumbria, CA16 6FA
Tel. 01768 351053
Fax/ISDN. 01768 353558
e-mail trans.pennine@virgin.net

Trans-Pennine are a
Quality Guild registered company

Reprographics
Barnabus Design & Repro
Threemilestone, Truro
Cornwall, TR4 9AN

And Printed in Cumbria by
Kent Valley Colour Printers
Shap Road Industrial Estate
Kendal, Cumbria LA9 6NZ

Cover picture: *Ullswater from Sharrow Bay, in the spring sunshine, revealing the lake's most beautiful face.* LE

Rear Cover Centre: *Howtown Bay from Martindale Hause, with the steamer* Raven *arriving with a load of passengers from Pooley Bridge.* AE

Rear Cover Top: *A spectacular view of a rainbow from outside the Old Church Hotel, which is just one of the amazing weather formations that occur on the lake.* DF

Rear Cover Bottom: *A Herdwick ewe and her lamb appreciate the solitude of Martindale, where the quiet roads are best explored on foot.* AE

Title Page: *Autumnal Ullswater from the Pooley Bridge landing stage, with its attractive reflections and powder blue sky.* AE.

THIS BOOK IS DEDICATED TO DOROTHY BERRY WHO SO LOVES ULLSWATER.

ISBN 0-9521070-2-3
British Cataloguing in Publication Data
A catalogue record for this book is available from the British Library

CONTENTS

ULLSWATER; AN INTRODUCTION

The three reaches of Ullswater seen looking north-east from Glencoyne Wood around the turn of the last century. CG

With its rugged shoreline and serpentine course, Ullswater is one of England's most spectacular lakes, and second largest to Lake Windermere located a few miles to the south-west. Situated entirely in the Lake District National Park, Ullswater is about 7.5 miles (12 km) long and 0.5 mile (0.8 km) wide, with an area of about 3 square miles (4.8 square km). In years past it was known as the 'Dark Lake', and legend connects it with King Arthur. It was always a place of mystery and myth, and in mediæval times monsters were believed to live in the dark still waters which have a maximum depth of 205 feet (62m). Whether this is the place where Arthur encountered the fabled Lady of The Lake will never be known, but one of the two steamers that ply Ullswater today is called thus.

Fed by streams from the high mountains, Ullswater is drained at its north-eastern end, by the River Eamont. In turn this joins the beautiful River Eden which changes the north-east flow of the Eamont, by heading north-west towards Carlisle beyond which it joins the Solway Firth where it turns west into the Irish Sea.

Helvellyn crowns Ullswater, at the south-western end of the valley. At 3,116 feet (950m) it is one of the most popular summits in the Lake District, because in the right weather conditions it is very accessible and central for most fell-walkers. Those who conquer the lofty summits will probably agree that Ullswater is one of the most beautiful of the Lakes.

Unfortunately (or fortunately, depending on your viewpoint) Ullswater is not the most frequently visited, despite its strong associations with William Wordsworth. He was one of the first to extol its beauty and his world famous poem 'Daffodils' is based on Ullswater. Sir Walter Scott was another who wrote of the lake, connecting it with the days of knights and chivalry when he penned the following words.

> He passed red Penrith's table round,
> For feats of chivalry renowned,
> Left Mayburgh's mound and stones of power,
> By Druids raised in magic hour,
> And traced the Eamont's winding way,
> Till Ulfo's lake beneath him lay.

Originally known as Ulfo's Water, Ullpha's Lake and Ulleswater, the lake today has all that could be desired by a modern traveller. The knight's horse may no longer be available, nor draughty castles and peasant huts, but good transportation and accommodation to suit all tastes and budgets is readily obtained. A regular bus service runs down the west side of the lake, whilst a post bus runs down the east side to Martindale. Along the lake itself a ferry service connects Pooley Bridge, Howtown and Glenridding during the season. Sailing, rowing and motor boats are all allowed on the Lake (subject to a 10mph speed limit) and, for the casual visitor, boats can also be rented by the hour during the summer months.

Windermere has all these and more but Ullswater undoubtedly has the better scenery and its wooded flanks are filled with a variety of wildlife, including the endangered red squirrel. As the lake heads south the fells begin to rise up to the skies, and in these golden eagles fly. On the skyline red deer may be seen scurrying away from the fall of your feet, and with the serpentine course of the lake down below who could want for more.

Fell walking and mountaineering are the big attractions today, and a prolifer-ation of really excellent walking guides point out the many wonderful excursions to be had. But even if you are following one of these guides, the fells should always be regarded with great respect. Without warning dark scudding skies can bring on a deluge in the valleys and a snowy blizzard on the tops.

As mentioned, there are many good hotels and bed & breakfast establishments overlooking the lake, several having spectacular views from their bedrooms. Glenridding, Patterdale and Pooley Bridge can supply you with food (to eat in or out) and hiking gear if you want to spend a day on the fells.

This book is not a walking guide, but an introduction to the area and its history, yet we would be remiss not to mention that fine walks can be enjoyed by all age groups and abilities. Perhaps the best of all family walks is that along the lakeside between Glenridding and Howtown, which should really be undertaken in connection with the steamer service.

There are far too many great walks to list them individually, but one of the Ordnance Survey maps or guide books on sale in local shops will give you a clue where to go. As a general guide it is worth mentioning that much of the lake shore is accessible and there are numerous paths leading up to the fells where the views get even better. So, whether you want to have a relaxing stroll to work off that huge breakfast or pub lunch, or if you are properly equipped and adequately prepared to tackle something more challenging you are sure to find a path to suit in this tremendously varied countryside.

Yet as you travel this spectacular valley, we are sure you will want to know more about the area. You will want to know about the communities and the people who live (and have lived) here and what they did.

The locals who welcome guests to their part of the world are hard-working folk, many of whom can trace their ancestry back for many centuries - some back to the Viking and Celtic days. They are a proud breed of people who have, in their own ways, been the real guardians of the Lake District. They were the guardians long before Canon Rawnsley helped to form the body which became the National Trust, and well before the formation of the National Park Authority. Many of them still farm the rugged uplands, and in these days when farming is in a crisis, they have a struggle to maintain the status quo. Most farmers welcome visitors to their land, but these visitors should always respect their way of life and the law of the countryside. So please, take only memories and leave only footprints!

In the pages that follow we will take you through the Ullswater area, introducing you to some of its places and some of its past characters. Yet we can be but brief, for the full story would fill many, many pages. From the days of King Arthur to Donald Campbell and his world water speed record, Ullswater has seen it all. Yet it remains largely unspoilt by the hand of man, and waits to beckon a new millennium where visitors and locals alike will never fail to appreciate its wondrous beauty!

FROM PENRITH TO PATTERDALE

The view down the lake from Waterfoot near Pooley Bridge looking towards Howtown, with the escarpment of Arthur's Pike and Swarth Fell on the left flank. AE

Ullswater may be said to lie in a glacial valley between Penrith and the Kirkstone Pass, along which the A592 road nowadays carries countless visitors through sylvan countryside. Indeed it is no idle claim to state that this is some of the finest countryside that the Lake District has to offer. Despite being just five miles from the bustling town of Penrith, the Ullswater valley is surprisingly serene and largely unspoilt by the modern ways of life. This chapter is based on the description of a journey from Penrith to Patterdale just as it would have been in the early days of travel to the lake, with a detour, which takes in the equally important Eamont valley.

Heading southward out of Penrith you cross the A66 and descend down Kemplay bank towards Eamont Bridge. This was the old boundary between Cumberland and Westmorland, and in years past was the scene of many skirmishes between warring factions. The name Kemplay comes from two distinct origins, the Danish (to wrestle) and the Saxon *ley* (field or meadow) and thus literally means place of battle or fighting.

The Eamont valley has supported many communities throughout the ages, and most of these will have crossed the river at its most accessible point where the present bridge now stands. The village has a rich history and some of the very ancient monuments that show this are mentioned elsewhere in this book. Alongside one of these historic sites (Arthur's Round Table), you leave the A6 on the B5320.

Heading past the pastoral villages of Yanwath and Tirril you go through the rich farmland of the ancient Barton parish, before arriving at Pooley Bridge. This point is the source of the River Eamont, and from the fine old bridge the lake comes into view. On the south-east shore is the road to Martindale, which will be described later.

Our route takes the opposite shore through the villages of Watermillock and Glenridding to Patterdale, and also passes the lovely park land of Gowbarrow and Glencoyne. The lake has two distinct 'dog-legs' in its form, between Howtown and the Gowbarrow area. At this point the lake's four named islands commence with the wooded Norfolk Island. The turning of the lake also affords some excellent views, and Glencoyne is really the only low-level point where the whole lake is visible.

The hills at the Patterdale end of the lake are far higher than those at the other end, so this results in a dramatic change in scenery in a very short distance. The main road follows the lakeshore for much of the way between Pooley Bridge and Glenridding, only venturing 'inland' to serve the villages or detour the grand houses that occupied the lake shore pastures before the road was built. Some of these houses are now attractive country hotels, and whilst it would be unfair to single out any one in particular, we can confidently say that many of them have very fine reputations indeed.

The main village on the side of the lake is Watermillock, but this is so well spread out that little of the settlement is seen from the road. What will be seen for much of the way are lake views on one side and the mountains slowly climbing to the west on the other. The main visitor attraction along the road is found at Aira Force, a magnificent waterfall situated between Gowbarrow and Glencoyne Parks. You will only see a car-park from the road, but this hides one of the most-famous features of the Lake District, and one that is well worth a visit.

A little beyond this point, and about a mile after the point where the A5091 descends from Troutbeck, is the National Trust's car park at Glencoyne Bridge. Running due east from here a remote valley climbs to Glencoyne Head, Sheffield Pike, Raise and Stybarrow Dodd below Helvellyn. Across the lake in the opposite direction Birk Fell and Silver Point will be seen.

An impressive feature a little further along is the spectacular cutting that was made in the rock to take the road round the base of Stybarrow Crag in the 1920s, to make a more direct route to Glenridding a little to the south.

Glenridding is the commercial heart of the Ullswater Valley, and it is the centre to which most tourists' head, but away from the bustle of the busy main street, it is the lake and open countryside that have so much more to offer.

Pressing on a short distance you will see the end of the lake, but it is easy to tell that Ullswater once went much further up the valley than it does today. The attractive Grisedale Beck is crossed in a little while, and then the road enters Patterdale, ostensibly the end of our journey. Yet the Patterdale valley beyond also forms an integral part of our story.

Like the valley of Ullswater, it was also formed in the Ice Age when the weight of the glaciers, many hundreds of feet thick, scraped the valleys out of the rugged mountain plateaux. The Patterdale valley is intersected by the Goldrill Beck that flows from Brothers Water into Ullswater. In turn the Goldrill is fed by a number of tributaries, including the Grisedale Beck, Deepdale Beck, Pasture Beck and Hayeswater Gill.

The last settlement of any size is found here in the beautiful village of Hartsop, a community that lies within walking distance of earlier settlements that date back many centuries. The road then begins its climb into the mountains, and beyond Brothers Water it heads up alongside the tumbling Kirkstone Beck, with the supposed remains of a Roman road on its opposite side. Beyond here is the summit of Kirkstone Pass, the great Helvellyn range, and the end of the Ullswater Valley, yet for many visitors this is just the start of their adventures.

Returning to Pooley Bridge, the more inquisitive visitor might wish to take the road to Howtown, but its narrow winding course and limited parking commends use of either the post bus or the lake steamer. In fact the road along the eastern shore really lends itself to a leisurely journey on foot or by cycle past camping sites and through some lovely countryside in the shadows of the fells. The lapping of the lake and the gentle clink of the rigging on the yachts moored offshore adds to the serenity. All the while the fells begin to rise higher and higher on the left. Askham Common leads on to Barton Fell, followed by Arthur's Pike, Bonscale Pike and Swarth Fell, with a sheer escarpment of scree slopes curving steeply up from the lakeside pastures.

Nearer Howtown, these scree slopes give way to grassy hillsides, and though seemingly inviting to walkers the climb is deceptive and Swarth Fell is best reached from nearby Fusedale. Hallin Fell near Howtown is well worth climbing, especially as the steep and winding Martindale Hause takes you part of the way.

Beyond the Hause (a steep hairpin road of alpine character), the valleys of Bannerdale and Boredale are a sight to behold. Their isolation means they are out of the range of many tourists, and are therefore peaceful, quiet and bathed in lovely sunshine when the weather obliges. These valleys are headed by the crags around Angle Tarn, but Boredale was once very busy when it served as the major trade route before the road down the western side of Ullswater was improved.

The road at Stybarrow in the 1930s. GH

A History Of Ullswater

ABOVE *If you want to get a real perspective on local history, and understand the extent of how far back it can be traced, then a walk on Askham Common is recommended. Here you will find a wealth of ancient sites, such as tumuli, cairns, stone circles and standing stones. In fact there can be little doubt that the Romans built their road (High Street) over this moor because it so clearly connected (and probably controlled) the ancient British settlements hereabouts. Several examples of standing stones can still be found, including the Cop Stone (probably a corruption of Cup Stone) seen here just off the track from Pooley Bridge to Heltondale.* AE

As it is impossible for us to trace the full and varied history of the Ullswater area, this section aims to set the scene on the area (which has witnessed the passing of many generations) by looking at the period from the Ice Age to the Vikings. Precisely who the first settlers were is not really known, but it is believed that man first came this way between four to five thousand years ago. They were probably migrant hunters, as those who later settled here needed skill to cope with the invariably harsh upland climate. From the end of the great ice age that carved out the area's physical characteristics, the high rugged mountains and the deep valleys have dominated the region.

These areas that we now know as fells and dales, both have names of Norse origin but although these terms are around 1,000 years old, they are relatively recent in the region's history. Long before the Vikings came sweeping into this rugged land, people had travelled through the area and there had been some transient settlement as well. The first people to settle permanently in the region were probably the dolio-cephalic race, more commonly known as the Polished Stone People who were then followed by the brachy-cephalic folk of the Bronze-age period.

For centuries little was known about these early settlers, but around Ullswater extensive traces of their habitation remained hidden. In the early 1930s, the Royal Commission for Historic Monuments appointed the geologist Thomas Hay to uncover the secrets behind ten old settlements that were known to exist beyond the head of Ullswater in the Patterdale valley.

In fact a series of ancient relics also run in a rough line along the escarpment between Askham and Martindale, and these also seem to indicate extensive early civilisation. The remains may appear insignificant today, but the sites are very old indeed. They take the form of a collection of at least a dozen cairns, burial circles and barrows (ancient and artificial mounds of stone or earth over a burial site). Perhaps the most significant is the stone circle known as the Cockpit on Askham Fell, and the circle near Lord's Seat just off High Street.

In at least five cases the excavation of sites around Arthur's Pike and Howtown has shown they date from the Bronze Age, between 4,000 and 2,000BC. However, as it is thought that barrows did not appear in Britain until c2,500BC, the date of these particular settlements may be just a mere 4,000 to 4,500 years old. The other settlements around Ullswater vary greatly in size and type, with some of considerable size (such as Millrigg), whilst others were barely big enough to have housed a single family. The larger ones were found near Hartsop Hall, Dale Head (in Bannerdale), Deepdale Bridge, and Glencoyne.

Many of the sites are noted for their location on 'morainic' ground, which is ground scattered with stone and other debris that came from the lines of rubble deposited by the Ice-age glaciers. Where the ancient walling of these settlements still exists, it is in a ruinous state, but still substantial enough to show the original thickness - four or five feet in most cases!

From an examination of the sites, the visitor will note no 'dressing' or splitting was undertaken by early stonemasons and only very rough stones were used, probably in the exact form that they were discovered on the hillside. The sites are situated between 550 and 1,000 feet above sea level and these heights vary according to their location in the valley.

Three of the five sites discovered in Glencoyne Park are at around 750 feet, while one at Deepdale is at 560 feet. The big one at Threlkeld is 1,000 feet, but the height of the settlements generally decreases the closer they come to Pooley Bridge, which is at the northeast, or lower end of Ullswater. The large number of sites that remain in such a small area indicates that a considerable amount of people probably lived around the lake and derived their living from hunting, fishing and herding. The lowest of the farmsteads was situated at 700 feet at Far Swan Beck in Glencoyne Park. A few of the old sites are linked with local folklore, with the best example being the Hartsop Hall settlement at the foot of the Kirkstone Pass. This site (not far from Deepdale Hall) is sometimes called the Druid Stones because of some very large erratic boulders left behind by the melting glaciers. Despite years of neglect this site still looks pretty impressive, with stones inside and outside the original boundary.

Near the village of Sandwick, a circular foundation can be found alongside an elaborate network of tracks. It is believed that these tracks originated from the time of the settlements themselves, and could have led to an old peat shelter on the edge of the fells. Some settlements have shown evidence of charcoal burning, a fact that made things a lot more difficult for the archaeologists, as it suggests that the sites may have had subsequent occupation in later periods. Nearly all the evidence of what really happened in the old settlements has been erased by centuries of neglect, and others were damaged because paths either crossed or came close to them.

Besides wall work, another feature at four of the Glencoyne settlements is that considerable work was done to build a battered embankment at the front, to provide a level platform behind it. Two of these sites have curious hollows, and one of the hollows must have taken a huge effort to dig out, as it is of considerable size. These features all indicate that these were permanent settlements and not ones established by merely nomadic visitors! A few years after the ten settlements were excavated; an eleventh site was found in Glencoyne Park, 850 feet up in the hills below Watermillock Common. It featured an outer wall and four telltale outlines of huts, one of which was partly built into the main wall. The settlement, which is close to Middle and Far Swan becks, is now affected by drainage problems and part of it is a real quagmire. That aside it is an impressive sight, and the foundations of its perimeter walls are still complete except, that is, for a gap on the uphill side where the entrance would have been.

In the days when these settlements were in use - dubbed the Neolithic 'lake-dwelling' period - the weather is believed to have been a lot warmer than it is nowadays. The scientific evidence that confirms this theory may be found in the remains of ancient trees in the peat and marshes of the hilltops where trees no longer tend to grow. Even so, walkers often find pieces of petrified wood while on their treks in the hills overlooking Ullswater and the other lakes. This is the legacy of the so-called 'Climatic Optimum' at the end of a 'mini' Ice age, possibly the original case of global warming!

It was with the arrival of the Celts, in particular the Cymri (also known as Cimmerie or Kumri), that the area became more permanently settled. These tribes bestowed their name upon the region, and down to the present day the word Cumbria bears mute testimony to their presence in this corner of England. Elsewhere in Cumbria, village names like Cumwhitton, Cumrew and Cummersdale, confirm the links.

There were frequent disputes over territory, until a dividing

ABOVE: *When the Cymri settled in the region, much of the valley floor area was little more than a steaming, swampy forest. Some built stilt houses in Ullswater and the lakes that then existed in the Eden Valley, which were probably very similar to this recreated example pictured on Lac du Chalain in the French Lake District.* AE

BELOW: *Here in Cumbria the permanent settlements tended to be on the hillsides above Ullswater and in the Pennines, such as that at Dale Head in Boredale. The Celts came to the region in two waves; the Hiberno-celts who came from the north and east, and the Cambro-celts who came from the south and west. Although they originated from the same region of Asia-minor (around the Caspian Sea), these two tribes did not settle in harmonious occupation of the region.* RK

line was established along the River Eamont and down Ullswater. With the Cambro-celts to the south of this line and the Hiberno-celts to the north, the pattern was set for what would eventually become the county boundary between Cumberland and Westmorland. Battles between the two tribes often took place, and one such encounter bestowed the name of Barco Hill (battle hill) on a site near Penrith. Other places that have Cymric origins can still be identified by names that have the words blen, pen, glen, cil (or gil), lyn and car within them. Thus Penrith, Glenridding, Carlisle, Blencowe, Helvellyn and so on, all show evidence of Celtic occupation. North of Ullswater the village of Catterlen, or *ceathir leana*, is an example of dual Hiberno-celtic and Cambro-celtic names.

These Celts brought with them their Mesopotamian religion, which was likely centred on the worship of the god Ba-al or Moloch and place names with bale, bel or bell, within them (eg. Bells Hill, Belmont), often have some direct connection with this primitive religion. Many sites around the area, such as Mayburgh Henge, Arthur's Round Table and so on, all link with this period of settlement. Yet these ancient Britons also had a significant part to play in the region's history and its subsequent folklore!

When the Romans arrived in the north they found the Brigantes occupying the Pennines, the Cymri in the Lakes and the Scots and Picts to the North. All were fierce and war-like! The outer limit of the Empire was established along the Clyde-Forth isthmus, but in due course the Roman forces in Scotland were ordered to fall back on the road/defence system between the Tyne & Solway. Hadrian built his famous wall alongside this line and, having held the war-like Scots behind this defensive system, the Romans tried to 'civilise' the British by emasculating them with luxury and vice. The Cymri and Brigantes resisted with force and guerrilla warfare, notably using the mountain areas for cover, but the Roman generals Agricola and Cerealis eventually won a decisive victory over the British in the wild wastes of Stainmore at the head of the nearby Eden Valley.

It was the Romans who began the real commercial exploitation of the area, and from their port at Ravenglass, they built a road through the heart of Lakeland cutting the British territory in half. This road, High Street, in turn connected with the Iter II (second highway) at Brougham. In addition to Iter II (which ran from York to Carlisle), other significant Roman roads are found within the area. One route that departed from Itter II, was the Maiden Way which carved a path across the Pennines into South Tynedale, and thus on to Hadrian's Wall. Yet another route went west to Keswick and possibly on to the Cumbrian coast. The important junction for these roads was *Brocavum* or Brougham, where a large civilian camp and military station was located at a bend on the River Eamont.

Soldiers from the border frontier were periodically rested here in rotation, forming a strategic reserve that could either be sent back to the wall or used to fortify the secondary defence line along Iter II if trouble arose. Major settlements or forts were built on this route (now the A66) at Bowes, Spittal, Roper Castle, Maiden Castle, Brough, Brackenber (near Appleby), Kirkby Thore, Brougham, *Voreda* near Plumpton (old Penrith) and Carlisle.

There is no firm date for when the Romans withdrew, but it seems that the Romano-British took an increasing level of control in local affairs between 400 and 420. The Roman historian, David Shotter writes 'it is not clear when Britain lost an institutional connection with the Roman empire' but then comments that 'after 402 no further supplies of money arrived to pay the army (or what was left of it).' So it was left to the British to take over the Roman infrastructure, and keep back the Scots, Irish and other invaders.

The roads themselves remained as busy trade routes, and along these would come European tribes such as the Angles and the Saxons. They came as traders at first, but later as invaders seeking to dispossess the British. It was actually the Romans who had forged these European links during the years of occupation, by their employment of Germanic mercenaries in the troubled Border areas. Indeed these foreign auxiliaries gave their name to many of the areas in which they settled, and the classic example is Dumfries (Fortress of the Friesians) just across the Solway Firth. Whilst many history books blame the vacillating King Vortigen for allowing the Saxons to settle in Britain in 428, it seems likely that the Saxon 'invasion' was a relatively peaceful affair at first. Later, as the British were forced to protect their homelands from conquest, the character Arthur Pendragon begins to appear in history and folklore.

No one knows who King Arthur was, or if he really existed at all, but there are scores of place names and legends that are connected with him all over Britain. Behind the myths and the fairy-tales lies a real story, but whether it refers to just one man or a group of men we may never know. The story tells the tale of how they tried to rescue what was left of Roman Britain from the invaders, but all the written evidence dates from a period long after Arthur is supposed to have lived. The main record of his feats and 12 major battles in the 5th and 6th centuries is to be found in a history written 400 years afterwards by the Welsh monk Nennius, but by this time the true facts might well have been considerably embellished. However, Arthurian legend has strong connections with Cumbria, and thus by extension, Ullswater. The three main areas to lay claim to Arthurian legend are Cumbria, Wales and Cornwall, and it may seem strange that all three should have such claims on one figure. But this anomaly might be logically explained by the fact that the Cymric tribe were forced out of Cumbria, retreating first to Wales and then to Cornwall.

Where Arthur lived, loved and fought can not be readily proved, but two of the sites can be firmly associated with the

North, these being Caledonian Woods and Camlann. The battle at Caledonian Woods was likely in Dumfriesshire, and almost certainly fought against Irish raiders who had landed on the Solway Firth. The site of the Battle of Camlann that took place in or around 515, and in which Arthur and Medraut (Sir Mordred) fell, is claimed by several places around the country.

The Arthurian Society firmly believe the location was near Camboglanna, close to the Roman fort on Hadrian's Wall at Birdoswald. If this is so, there may be some substance in the suggestion that *Merrie Carlisle* was Arthur's Camelot and that the small church at Arthuret near Longtown is his burial place. Furthermore, in the Mallerstang Valley and near the head of the Eden Valley stands Pendragon Castle (reputedly the home of Uther Pendragon - King Arthur's father). This ancient castle is perhaps one of the most tangible signs of the connection despite its most ruinous state.

According to legend, on his death Arthur was transported to *Avalon*, meaning 'the place of Apples'. One theory places Avalon on an island in the Solway Firth Marshes near Burgh-by-Sands, and the small Roman fort in the nearby village was certainly known as *Aballave* (Apple Orchard). Furthermore, it is not far from the site of the burial place of another English monarch, Edward I, whose memorial can still be seen on the wild and desolate marshes.

A more remote suggestion is that Arthur was laid to rest on an island in the mist-shrouded lake that once lay near Appleby-in-Westmorland in the Eden Valley.

For the Arthurian Society, the growing feeling is that after being mortally wounded, Arthur was taken to a small fort near the River Esk, and after his death his head was severed from his body and laid in the ground at Arthuret. Whatever the case concerning Arthur, there can be little doubt that Cumbria, by then almost a free state, was the scene of considerable trouble.

It was soon established as the British kingdom of Rheged, which lasted between the 5th and 7th centuries. Based on the Eden Valley, Carlisle and Alston Moor, it reached its height under King Urien (or Urbgen), when Rheged stretched from Strathclyde to Lancashire. With his champion, Gwallaig, Urien kept the Bernician Engles back in Northumbria for many years, but he was finally killed by an assassin during the siege of Lindisfarne

Pendragon Castle

in 590. His son, Owien is incorporated in the Arthurian legends as a prominent Knight of the Round Table. Yet this history is not forgotten, and it will form a permanent feature in the new £12million visitor and interpretation centre at Slapestones on the junction of the A66 and A592,

The colonisation by the Angles, Saxons and Jutes (the English) had begun in earnest around 547, when King Ida of Bernicia landed his forces in Northumbria. A major battle at *Catraeth* (probably Catterick) saw the defeat of the combined British tribes in 570 and the English began their domination of the north. Yet, in the period 572-3 the combined British won a tremendous series of victories against Ida's son Theodric, whose English forces were pushed right back to the Northumbrian coast and thereafter kept at bay by the Cumbrians.

The last pagan Saxon king Æthelfrith (593-616) was a superb military tactician, and he began a campaign to re-establish English superiority. In 603 he dealt with the threat from the Scots and all-but annihilated the army of their king Ædan Mac Gabran at Degsaston.

After dealing with the Scots, he contrived a mass advance into the heart of British territory and set up his battle camp near the main Celtic stronghold at Chester. This bold move was intended to demoralise the Britons once and for all, and drive a wedge between the British settlements in the west. He certainly succeeded in forcing the British deep into Powys in Wales, but it is strange that the English did not continue their advance against the Britons now isolated in Cumbria. Perhaps this was because the Lakes mountains proved to be just too great an obstacle, and they were certainly suited to 'guerrilla warfare'.

Whatever the reason, the Britons remained almost totally isolated for many years, a position that continued until the battle of Deniseburna just south of Hexham, where the British cause was finally defeated in the North. By 670 almost all of Cumbria was inside the Northumbrian Kingdom, and places like Inglewood Forest (Angle wood) bear witness to the English presence hereabouts. However, before long the English in turn were to be threatened by the Vikings. During the 9th century the Danish began raiding the Tyne-Solway Gap with a vengeance, ruining much of Hexham and Carlisle.

In 915 the English were routed at the battle of Corbridge and the Vikings swept into Cumbria. Evidences of their conquest

The view from Dobbin Wood to Sandwick, which is essentially the same now as it has been for centuries. AE

are to be found, but it is in the many Viking place-names that remain in the Lakes that we find the greatest evidence; places such as Sandwick, Holm Thorpe, Thwaites, and the like. Names of natural features also give us similar evidence, with foss or force for waterfall, fell for hill and wath for ford. There was an uneasy peace between Saxon and Viking in Cumbria, until Æthelstan finally received the surrender of all the Kings of England at Dacre Castle on the banks of the River Eamont near Penrith in 930. But even then the era was not a peaceful one, with wars being waged with the Scots and malcontent factions of the supposedly 'united' English.

To resolve the border between the Viking lands and the Scottish kingdom of Strathclyde (which by then included Cumbria), King Edmund erected Rey Cross on Stainmore and at this religious symbol, both kings swore an oath to God that they would not cross the boundary with war-like intent. Yet at this very place in 954, the traitor Ewl Maccus killed the last Danish king of York, Eric Bloodaxe, after his force had been trapped by converging armies. Ironically, this military manoeuvre was an almost identical tactic to the Roman pincer movement that had cornered the Brigantes at the same spot almost nine centuries earlier.

However the Danes were not finished, and in 966, Thored, son of Gunnar laid waste to the whole of Westmorland, as well as the Eden Valley, and possibly Alston Moor. In 1000 it was the turn of the English to strike under Ethelred, and they in turn attacked and destroyed the large Danish colonies in the area re-establishing their own systems and cultures. Within a century, yet another invader struck north along the old Roman roads in an attempt to subdue the unsettled border and resolve the territorial disputes with Scotland.

After the arrival of the Norman forces in 1066 William the Conqueror's son, William Rufus, went north to subdue the border taking possession of Carlisle in 1092 and establishing forts at strategic points along the route from York. First timber buildings were erected as a temporary measure, but these were soon followed by the magnificent stone structures, many of which (like Appleby Castle) remain today. The Norse culture was thus finally subdued and today very little remains of Ullswater's Viking settlements, other than the place names. Their old long houses have long since perished or been burnt away by the settlers who followed! Even so, for those who are interested, examples of these Wattle houses, made using interlaced twigs or branches (in panels) can be seen recreated in the Jorvik Museum at York.

*NB: All dates quoted in numerals are anno domini dates.

A LAKE FOR ALL SEASONS

An imposing view down Ullswater on the path descending from St. Sunday Crag to Birks. RK

The lake and surroundings of Ullswater are noted as among the best scenery in Britain, or even the world, a fact not lost on the poet William Wordsworth when he visited the area as a youth of 18 in 1788. It was to have a great impression on his life, as we know so well today. Similarly, the guidebook author Alfred Wainwright was in awe of the landscape on his first Lakeland holiday in 1930. What started as just another routine holiday changed Wainwright's life, but it would also result in literary history and inspire generations of walkers and country-lovers for years to come. In their own way, both of these men extolled the beauty of Ullswater, and their literature is widely available in the area today.

If you come and look around the Ullswater valley yourself you will soon see why it has so inspired artists, poets and romantics for at least two centuries! However, the awe-inspiring countryside around the lake should not be taken for granted, and its geology is worthy of consideration, for this affected all that would follow. Although much of what we see today is either pasture or moor land, years ago it was virtually all forest. The deforestation began here around 2,000 years before Christ, when the first settlers decided they needed to make a living by subsistence farming, and the first clearings were made in the vast forests. Livestock grazing and later crop cultivation all took their toll and the forests diminished in size.

The geology of the Lake District is a fascinating and absorbing subject and far beyond the scope of this book; yet we should briefly mention how the area was formed. Basically the Lake District is made up from three broad bands of rock which trend from the south west to the north east. The oldest group are the Skiddaw Group rocks that were formed as a black mud settling in a deep sea in the Ordovician period around 500,000,000 years ago. Then came the Borrowdale Volcanic Group of rocks which formed as a huge volcanic island after lava erupted in a pyroclastic flow later in the Ordovician period (around 450,000,000 years ago). The lava then cooled to form very hard rocks, mainly Andesite but also Basalt and Rhyolite. The third band came in the Silurian period around 420,000,000 years ago when a range of slates and sandstones were formed into what we geologists call the Windermere Group.

Around 400,000,000 years ago all three bands of rock were folded and faulted as two continental plates collided. These faults were then intruded by flows of molten magma and lifted up to form an exceptionally high mountain range. This event is called the Caledonian Orogeny, and the resulting mountains would not have been dissimilar to the Himalayas that were formed when the Asian and Indian continents collided. As a result of this folding many of the Borrowdale rocks were compressed, and this in turn created the famous Westmorland green slates that are so common in walls and buildings all around the Lake District National Park.

Erosion over millions of years wore down these mountains, and then they sank beneath a tropical sea in the Devonian period about 350,000,000 years ago. This sea teemed with life, including snails, crinoids, brachiopods, corals and so on. As these creatures died, their shells littered the sea bed, and a thick layer of debris eventually built up to form the pale grey rocks known as Carboniferous Limestone. Remains of these creatures can still be commonly found in the rocks today!

As the millenniums went by, the sea became filled with mud, sand and grit, and as the ground mass uplifted once again, swampy forests began to grow. This became known as the Carboniferous period, and on the fringes of the Lake District deep coal measures duly formed. Around 280,000,000 years ago, yet another period of folding and uplifting took place in what we now call the Hercynian Orogeny. The dome that this uplifting formed was also worn away by erosion, and today the carboniferous limestone is usually just a rim along the edge of the older mountain formations.

Since the Ordovician period, the part of the earth's crust that now makes up the Lake District had been moving north from the southern hemisphere. Around 250,000,000 years ago, the Lakeland landmass reached the latitude of the present day Sahara. As a consequence desert conditions existed, and the rich red sandstone of the Eden Valley was formed.

This took us through the Permian and Triassic periods (which ended around 190,000,00 years ago), when shallow, salty lakes were formed amidst the sand dunes. Yet all the time the tectonic plate, on which the Lakeland rocks stood, was moving north and slightly westward.

During the time from the earth's creation onward, the globe had been rapidly cooling as the crust expanded and solidified. The climate continued to cool down, and around 2,000,000 years ago snow and ice began to accumulate on the summits of the Lakeland mountains. Glaciers formed, and these built up over the centuries gradually spreading across the country. During warmer spells, called inter-glacials, the ice melted and the glaciers retreated, only to re-emerge as another period of cooling began. With the constant movement of these huge masses of ice, the landmass was scoured and huge valleys and rugged glacial features appeared. Cirques, aretes, glacial troughs and finger lakes were all created, and the Ullswater Valley has classic examples of each type - the most distinctive being Ullswater, itself a giant finger lake!

When the climate finally warmed up again the glaciers progressively retreated and melt-water formed the lakes. These waters may be generally divided into two types, mesotrophic lakes and oligotrophic lakes, of which Ullswater falls into the latter category. In time life was re-established in the lakes as their temperatures rose, but several of them contain fish that date from the immediate post-ice age. As far as Ullswater is concerned its rare inhabitant is a white fish called the *Coregonus lavaretus*, which is more commonly known by its norse name of schelly. This ice age fish has a distinct Celtic connection (the Celts actually called it the gwyniad or powan) and whilst it is discovered in only a few select lakes today, the other places to provide a habitat are found in the other Celtic lands of Wales and Scotland. Other types of fish migrated to the lake when the water temperatures eventually rose. Yet more were introduced (possibly by the Romans) when fishing became an early industry on Ullswaterside. By the 17th century fishing had turned into a sport, and when James Clarke wrote his *Survey of The Lakes* (1787), he commented that he had caught no less than 29 fine trout during one trip.

The schelly were still thriving when Clarke had his angling session but in this century their numbers began to dwindle, mainly in connection with pollutant materials such as lead waste or oil entering the lake. Large numbers of schelly were washed up dead in 1939 and 1977, but the reason for this was never fully determined. Since then these 'ancient' fish have been struggling for survival although modern initiatives are now being taken to ensure their preservation. Other shoals of schelly are quite uniquely found in Red Tarn (a mesotrophic lake) in the shadow of Helvellyn, but one old angling book commented that these were 'nowhere near as tasty as their brethren in Ullswater as the fish have an insipid taste.'

Although Ullswater is one of the larger lakes, more like Windermere and with similar surroundings, there is a curious absence of fish such as pike and char. The char became 'extinct' by 1872, with the waste from the local lead-mining industry being blamed for their demise, while evidence suggests pike were never in Ullswater to begin with.

The Ullswater area is a comparatively dry part of the Lake District, but even so the weather can turn on you spectacularly sometimes when you don't expect it. Our later chapter on the work of the Mountain Rescue Team at Patterdale will also show the consequences. The Kepple Cove Dam disaster of 1927 (which devastated Glenridding in just half an hour following a violent storm), and a waterspout reported on the lake near Glencoyne Park in 1953 are just a couple of examples of the vagaries of the weather. In fact the Meteorological Office records show that the Pooley Bridge area receives around 60 inches of precipitation a year. Yet, just a few miles further into the higher area beyond Glenridding and Patterdale, this can exceed 100 inches on average. But even so this does not compare with the 200 inches or so, which fall in the Borrowdale valley, and that is only a few miles to the north-west 'as the crow flies'.

The fact that Cumbria is the wettest area in England, and one of the wettest in the whole of Britain, just shows how unpredictable the weather can be. In turn this is a fact that has influenced life in the area for many years past and one that can still catch out the unwary today. Visitors to the Ullswater area have certainly suffered because of the weather, despite the season, as the following accounts will show.

TOP RIGHT: *Despite the ever present threat that winter has not quite departed from the area, spring is a time of awakening, and a time when snowdrops, daffodils and baby lambs appear. It holds out a hope that better days are just ahead, and it can offer some remarkably warm and sunny days even in March. It is also an optimistic time, as the promise of warmer weather brings an influx of visitors like these walkers starting out on the path from Howtown to Sandwick.* AE

BOTTOM RIGHT: *Spring is traditionally the busiest time of the year, and whilst it can be a pleasant time to explore the Lake District you still need to be wary. For example, even the great speed ace Donald Campbell was caught out by the weather as he prepared for his world water-speed record with Bluebird on Ullswater, when his speed and reliability trials were held up in March 1955 by some particularly vicious snowstorms. Our picture shows the boat at Glenridding as it is being pulled from the water by a David Brown 'Taskmaster' tractor especially loaned to Campbell for the speed attempt.* DBT

High summer on Ullswater from Boncsale Pike. RK

Autumn turns to winter looking across the lake from Gowbarrow. RK

Perhaps the most dramatic springtime incident in recent times was recorded on the lake during a spectacular rescue in 1961. It happened as two inexperienced sailors were out on the lake in a small dinghy and were caught out by a strong gust. Without warning the strong gale blew down Ullswater on the last Sunday in March and the sailing dinghy capsized in the choppy water. The crew struggled in the icy water for over an hour, but a motor boat raced to the rescue in horrendous conditions. The water was so wild that even this boat was out of sight from the shore at times, and the dozens of people watching helplessly from shore thought it had sunk. However, the stricken sailors were finally reached and the first one was pulled aboard via the boarding ladder at the stern, but the second was caught in the propeller and badly injured.

In addition to the bad times, there are the good times also, and there have been very mild winters and quite spectacular summers. The year 1946 was a memorable one, and as the Lake's water level dropped one of the steamers actually grounded at its moorings. Another prolonged spell of warm weather during the gorgeous summer of 1976 reduced the waterfall at Aira Force to a mere trickle

The high point in recent years was 1995, when the skies were nearly cloudless and temperatures soared to more than 80° Fahrenheit (27°C.) at times. In recent years the warm summers like these have led to a very high demand for water in the North West. As a consequence the water levels of Ullswater and nearby Haweswater have been reduced in order to top up the water supply network.

A springtime view from Howtown to Hallin Fell, with 'Wordsworth's Daffodils' inset. AE

RIGHT: *Not far from Ullswater, and just over the High Street ridge, is the Haweswater valley. Flooded in the 1930s to provide water for Manchester, the former village of Mardale usually lies 20 to 30 feet below the surface of the waters. Only a tiny island, Wood Howe, the top of a former hill at the edge of the village normally betrays its location. But occasionally, the weather is so dry that the remains of the old village re-emerge (as shown here), and Mardale becomes a tourist attraction. In 1973, 1984 and 1995 the village has appeared from beneath the waves, and visitors have flocked down to walk over the old pack-horse bridge, and stroll among the walled lanes of this forgotten village. Other things emerge too, as for example an old safe, which was discovered in the 1995 drought, after it had been dumped in the lake following a robbery !* AE

For many visitors the Lakes are at their finest when the rich Autumn colours of the golden trees are reflected in the water. Although the weather gets progressively less stable, autumn really is one of the best times to visit, quiet roads, fine lakeside walks and beckoning pub fireplaces feature as we head out of British Summer Time. This season has a few stories of its own to tell, but none are more hilarious than the one when the national press made a fool of itself in October 1946. Following a blazing hot summer, the weather deteriorated rapidly and autumn was a time of serious flooding all round Britain. For some reason several of the national newspapers took it on themselves to suggest that Brotherswater and Ullswater had 'joined' because of the floods. If true this would have been a slight problem for communities around Ullswater as the other lake is at least 35 feet (10.7 metres) higher in altitude.

Yet autumn can be very warm too, and in November 1946 a freak heat-wave sent temperatures soaring toward 70° Fahrenheit (21°C) across Cumbria, tempting the tourists to hit the road again. Further floods hit the area in the autumn of 1951, when they overwhelmed the pumps at the Greenside Lead Mines and flooded the workings. There were also bad floods in 1954 and 1962, whilst recent autumn storms have caused the lake to flow over the road in places. Yet even in the rain and blustering winds of autumn, the colours of Ullswater are more than enough to provide a memorable holiday and help one prepare for the dark winter months ahead.

Winter is a time of spectacular beauty, but also one of great danger both in the fells and on the lakes. It is traditionally a time of hardship for the local farming community, and even the hardy sheep breeds like Swaledales and Herdwicks can suffer dreadfully when caught on the exposed uplands. Many can find shelter and survive, but it is not an uncommon sight to see upland farmers trudging through deep snow drifts to rescue their flocks or take out food to them.

One of the worst winters was that experienced in 1607/8, which is listed in the *Guinness Book of Records* as one of the harshest winters Britain has known. The great freeze of nearly 400 years ago was at its worst nationally between 5th December and 14th February, but records for Watermillock suggest the frosts began as early as 1st September. It finally abated on 22nd February when the Lake thawed and shed the slab of ice that had been its surface since 6th December. Between these dates farmers would take their sheep across the frozen lake between Pooley and Sharrow Sands rather than trudge with them over snowbound fields and tracks. Horse loads of corn and barley were taken over the ice to all the villages on the lake in order to feed the locals and their animals. Then, on 6th January 1608, several young people from the Soulby Fell area held an afternoon-long dancing party on the frozen surface. On 9th February the locals around Watermillock celebrated Shrove Tuesday, by lighting a bonfire on the ice and having shooting and marksmanship contests.

The next bleak winter was the one recorded for 1894-95, and on 16th February 1895 the *Cumberland & Westmorland Herald* carried the story: 'SPLENDID SKATING ON ULLSWATER - NEARLY NINE MILES OF ICE'. Another report was of 'A SAD ACCIDENT' which referred to an incident when Captain Holmes, the master of the steamer *Raven*, went missing after setting off to skate between Glenridding and his home in Pooley Bridge. That tragedy aside, the lake was regularly a scene of great activity as crowds of skaters took to the ice day after day, and some (rather foolhardily) at night. Thousands of people braved hazardous roads or long train journeys (including visitors from Manchester, Newcastle and London) just to see the lake and skate on it that weekend. Then on the Thursday afternoon, Valentine's Day, around 500 people from the Penrith area took advantage of 'half-day closing' and headed for the ice.

In more recent memory the winter of 1963 was the year most people will recall today. Several in this area say it was even worse than the bad winter of 1946/7 which records show was actually at its worst in the Pennine hills east of Penrith. A major story from 1963 was the 'RELIEF OF MARTINDALE'. This covered the isolation of the communities in the two remote valleys beyond Howtown, and how supplies were taken in for people and animals trapped without food. It also reported how a pregnant woman was air-lifted by the then novel use of a helicopter after she went into labour.

Whilst the snow was trying its best to bury the traffic on the roads around Watermillock (including one trapped bus), a bizarre prank took place on the lake. In this remarkably stupid incident a 27 year-old 3-wheeler car (which was probably a 1936 Morgan) was set off across the lake without a driver for a joke. It went for over a mile from Gale Bay to Flosh Gate, twisting and turning yet narrowly dodged the 50 or so skaters milling around on the ice.

On several occasions, most notably in 1929, 1947, 1962, 1963, and 1979 Aira Force waterfall has been pictured in local newspapers almost completely frozen. Yet it is not just this hugely-popular tourist attraction that occasionally catches a 'cold', as many of the streams and waterfalls turn into cascades of shimmering ice. Yet despite the beauty of it all, it is a hard time for animals. For example, in February 1952 a sheep was trapped in a waterfall on Swarthbeck Gill at the foot of Arthur's Pike. There it was stuck for 26 days, but it was remarkably rescued alive. Its only ailment was a dead-leg, but once the circulation to the limb had been restored, the sheep was happily running around on all-fours, none the worse for its experience. Another animal in trouble was Hedy, a spaniel belonging to the famous Ullswater hotelier Brian Slack. This was rescued from the snow in 1955 by a keen climber and local solicitor, the late-C. Eric Arnison, who later received an award for his actions.

Sadly, some rescue attempts do not have satisfying end results, as shown in the snowy Easter of 1951 when a group of mountaineers set out to tackle the fells, ill-prepared for what could happen. After tragedy ensued and one of them died from exposure, the local coroner was compelled to warn climbers to expect the worst! Almost 50 years on, those words of warning are sometimes tragically forgotten as we will discuss later when we consider the work of the Patterdale Mountain Rescue Team!

WHERE TO FIND HELP & ADVICE

In presenting an overview of the climatic vagaries of the Ullswater area, we hope the visitor will appreciate its many hidden dangers. Yet as the Lake District National Park Authority warn 'each year there are accidents which could have been avoided. Make sure you enjoy your activities by observing basic safety advice.'

To provide that advice, the Authority produce a number of information leaflets notably:

'Safety On The Fells'
and
'Safety On The Water'.

The Lake District National Park Authority also operate a free advisory service for fell walkers and boat owners (including registration) which are provided from the

RANGER SERVICE   **01539 724555**
WEATHER FORECAST SERVICE   **017687 75757**

Alternatively, call at the
National Park Information Offices at:
The Square, Pooley Bridge   **017684 86530**
and
Beckside Car Park, Glenridding   **017684 82414**

The head offices of the Lake District National Park Authority are:
Murley Moss, Oxenholme Road, Kendal, Cumbria LA9 7RL where a 24-hr. voice mail service is provided on:- **01539 724555**

In Penrith, Eden District Council provide a tourist information centre at Robinson's School, Middlegate, Penrith CA11 7PT   **01768 867466**.

The Cumbria Tourist Board are based at:
Ashleigh, Holly Road, Windermere and can assist with more specialist enquiries, although you should always try to contact the local information centres first.   **015394 44444**

IN CASE OF EMERGENCY
The mountain rescue and lake rescue services should be alerted by dialling **999** and asking for **POLICE**, who will in turn alert the appropriate rescue service.

THE LAKE

A spring view across the lake from Sharrow Bay. LE

The water level for Ullswater is around 475 feet (145m) above sea level, and this remarkable lake has seen many uses and one or two battles, not all of which were back in the days of history as we will see. Boats have been seen on the lake for centuries, and the Cymri tribesmen would have used their little walnut-shell shaped boats, akin to the Welsh Coracles, both for fishing and crossing the lake. The Romans made much use of water-borne transport, and they would probably have used the lake in some form or another, if only for gathering fish - a staple part of the Roman diet. The suggestion that a Roman causeway went down to Glencoyne Bay, may indicate that this linked into some sort of boat service.

The Danes undoubtedly had vessels on Ullswater, and possibly small versions of their longships would have been tied up in Sandwick bay or at other points along the shore. In mediæval times there was some considerable level of traffic on the lake and it is believed that a ferry operated across the lake between Aira Beck and Howtown Bay. Yet in more modern times we associate the greater use of the lake as a leisure resource. Arthur Ransome's novel, *Swallows and Amazons* certainly gave popularity to boating on the lake, but all manner of craft have plied its waters. Ranging from crude wooden rafts to paddle steamers and from luxury cabin cruisers to wind-surfing boards Ullswater has seen them all.

Many of the earliest 'pleasure' boats were those owned by the more prosperous people who built country homes around Patterdale and Watermillock. As time progressed many of them had their own steam launches to convey them around the Lake. Yet it was not only for pleasure that vessels took to the Lake, and with the expansion of the lead mining industry a lot more use was made of Ullswater. Effectively the lake was the primary means of moving supplies down the valley, and as mining developed at Greenside the tiny hamlet of Glenridding suddenly grew beyond all recognition. The demand for transport from those who settled in the upper end of the valley, along with the growing numbers of tourists, led to the founding of the steamer service from 1859 onwards.

Another boat once connected with tourism was an 8-oared rowing boat that operated from Pooley Bridge in the 1780s. Nothing unusual in that you may think, but this boat had a few little extras that set it apart from all the other craft on Ullswater as large brass swivel-guns were used to 'try the echoes' around the lake and surrounding fells. This 'gunboat' must certainly have shattered the peace, but the 12 or 13 echoes that it could achieve were very popular with the tourists.

The next major travel idea for Ullswater came in the 1870s when a railway was proposed to link Pooley Bridge to Penrith. Even though no railway was ever constructed to bridge the five mile gap, more and more visitors began arriving at the Lake as the 20th century dawned. A local printing firm (Reeds) began producing fine Ullswater tourist guides before the Great War, and the 1912 edition carried advertisements for a wide variety of services. Yet, with the demands for water-based tourism growing, pressures were beginning to be placed on the environment. As this tourism began to bring in much needed money it took a bold move in the 1920s to present the warning that the Lake District needed careful development.

The formation of a statutory body to protect the area was destined to take many years, but the dream finally became a reality in 1951 when 'National Park' status was achieved. The 'Park' concept was seriously promoted in October 1929, when it was discussed at the Manchester conference of the Council for the Protection of Rural England which attracted Viscount Ullswater among others. This conference set things in motion and by June 1934, the Friends of The Lake District got together to fight their corner in the battle to preserve the area's charm, with the blessing of the then Prime Minister Ramsay McDonald.

One of the biggest problems that the environmentalists would face was the issue of pollution. Just before World War II a lot of the blame for this problem in the Lakes was placed on the operators of speedboats, with their being accused of spilling oil into the lake thus killing its fish and wildlife. Whatever the cause, real problems were developing and some visitors justifiably complained that the Lake was 'filthy'. Yet at that time there was little opportunity to resolve matters.

ABOVE: *Ullswater experiences quite varied weather phenomenons, but few are as unusual as this freak storm caught on film looking towards Scalehow Force waterfall in the autumn of 1996. NT*

BELOW: *The promise that winter is drawing to an end is always associated with new life. In this view a Herdwick ewe continues another cycle of life with the next generation. LE*

The war intervened and Ullswater was put to other uses, including the testing of naval craft, miniature submarines and the odd flying boat, whilst the army practiced in the hills around the area. So things did not get any better!

Peacetime brought a demand for greater leisure use, and 20 years on, the problem of speed boats got worse and worse. In the red-hot summer of 1976 the nuisance reached a pinnacle and a campaign to impose a speed limit was launched, but in February 2,000 people (many of whom were skiers) protested to the Secretary of the State for the Environment, Anthony Crosland. They must have been hopeful of success when the inquiry into the matter began in June, but a serious accident to a speedboat with a skier in tow only a month later began to turn public opinion against them. This incident happened when the boat ran aground on rocks near Place Fell, severely injuring the driver and leaving two girl passengers hurt.

In September the campaigners for the speed limit 'wheeled in the big guns' to help the cause; the film giants Lord Olivier and Sir Alec Guinness, and the novelist-critic J. B. Priestley all visited Ullswater to add their names to the '10mph club'. In July 1983, the Ullswater Ski-ing Club and their supporters finally lost their case when the new limit came into force.

Another serious problem that has faced Ullswater over the years has been the continual threat of water extraction, notably due to the former Manchester Corporation who demonstrated an insatiable demand for H_2O. Not content with exploiting Thirlmere and flooding the Haweswater Valley, they also went for Ullswater in a big way. The first chapter in this long saga was the creation of the Thirlmere Reservoir, which came on-stream in October 1894. However, as the city kept growing and becoming ever more prosperous, it was then recognised that even Thirlmere was going to be inadequate for the demand. Therefore, in 1907 the Haweswater valley to the east of Ullswater was earmarked for a new reservoir.

The villagers of Mardale Green were horrified at the news, and a lengthy campaign was waged against Manchester Corporation over several years. Yet, in these days there was no protection for the lakes and in the first weeks of 1929, defeat had to be conceded when 'workers' huts were put up at the lower end of the natural Hawes-water and work on building the reservoir and a huge aqueduct tunnel began.

The Haweswater dam was completed in 1940 but only nine years later, Manchester was back for more. In June 1949 they announced a new scheme to 'tap' Ullswater, and thus began a battle which would rumble on through the 1950s. Then, in October 1961 Manchester Corporation was presented with a petition carrying around half-a-million signatures in protest against the Ullswater scheme. The 'Lakes' Great Advocate', Lord Birkett of Ulverston, joined the case for Ullswater as the battle raged on, and another petition was sent on behalf of Ullswater in January 1962.

As with the Wet Sleddale project (near Shap), however, another 500,000 signatures looked set to be ignored, but this time the matter was raised in the House of Lords by Lord Birkett. The debate on 8th February lasted seven and a half hours, but It resulted in a vote of 70 to 36 against the scheme.

Sadly, the debate had taken a great deal out of Lord Birkett, and the following day he fell ill and was rushed to the London Clinic but to no avail. Shocked at his sudden death, members of the Ullswater Preservation Society called for one of the local hills, Nameless Fell, to be named in honour of him.

Yet, like the proverbial bad penny, Manchester came back again. Even after W. M. F. Vane, the MP for Westmorland, successfully had the project voted out yet again in 1963, it was not over. The following year the Ullswater Preservation Society set up a 'fighting fund' to continue their campaign against the Corporation, and also held a poll to find out what local people thought. The results were, for Manchester 3 votes, against 30,000, figures that still speak for themselves.

The next move for the Ullswater Preservation Society was to ask Dan Smith, Chairman of the recently founded Northern Economic Planning Council, to fight their cause. Smith could clearly see what troubles the Ullswater community were facing, and in January 1966 he also alerted them to the dangers of ignoring the potential of the M6 motorway that was being built at the time. He also told Ullswater folk that they should start drawing up plans to attract visitors once the motorway arrived, for fear that tourists would just fly past and ignore the Lakes as a destination for their holidays.

When the crunch came, it came suddenly for on 6th May 1966, the result nobody in Lakeland wanted to hear was announced - Manchester Corporation had finally got its way! Richard Crossman, the Minister for Housing and Local Government finally gave the Mancunians permission to take water from Ullswater and Windermere. He said he was reluctantly giving the go-ahead, although he had 'done all he could to protect Ullswater, by putting in stringent safeguards to stop the Corporation taking too much water from the lake.'

A special weir was to be built to prevent excessive amounts of water from being taken, and the limit would be set at 25 million gallons a day. Furthermore, if the lake surface fell below the height of 475 feet 6 inches above sea level, the Corporation could not extract a single drop from Ullswater.

Even this was not the end of demands on Ullswater and yet another reservoir was suggested for Howe Grain Beck in Bannerdale. Fortunately this desecration of the landscape never came to be, but during the record drought of 1995 when Haweswater was down to only 11% of its capacity, a pumping station was erected at Pooley Bridge alongside a temporary weir built across the mouth of the Eamont. Then, amid great debate water was pumped out of Ullswater to slake the thirst of the parched North West.

Donald Campbell and The Ullswater Speed Record

In June 1954 there was great excitement in the district when Donald Campbell, the famous speed king, visited Ullswater. He came to assess the lake for a new World Water-Speed Record and before the year was out a new boathouse had been built on the shore near Glenridding Pier. Then, in January 1955 his boat *Bluebird K-7* arrived and Campbell's mechanic Leo Villa started to get it ready for the initial trials, but these were badly disrupted by the aforementioned bad weather in March.

After a long build up, Campbell (aged 34) finally climbed aboard his craft, destined to make history on Saturday, 23rd July 1955. He shot down the lake in *Bluebird* on what was said to be another trial run, but he clocked the 'measured kilometre' at 215.08 mph (346.15 km/h). After turning round, with crowds and the entire world media looking on, he decided to make it official.

Returning at 189.57 mph (305.08 km/h), the new record was firmly established at an average of 202.32 miles (325.61 kilometres) per hour. This beat the record, set by Stanley Sayres in America in 1950, by 24mph. Yet, Campbell modestly said that the first record of over 200 miles per hour, was all down to 'Leo and the boys - my part has been small by comparison.' Afterwards he had to be helped out of the cockpit because an old back injury had been aggravated in these latest runs, but his wife Dorothy and his mother Lady Campbell embraced him in front of the cheering crowd. Today he is still remembered with affection on Ullswater, and a display of Campbell memorabilia can be found at the Glenridding Hotel.

But this was the last of the Ullswater record attempts, and as transport historian Professor Alan Earnshaw notes:- 'Coniston seemed a better bet as Campbell aimed for the magic 250 mph. In the four years from 1956 to 1959 he set four records on Coniston. Then in 1964 he set the land record at 403.1 mph on the bed of Lake Ayre, and on New Year's Eve that year he achieved 276.33mph on Lake Dumbleyung. Both these records were set in Australia, but he remains the only man ever to gain both the water and land speed records in the same year.

In 1967 Lee Taylor bettered the water record by 9mph on Lake Gunterville in the USA. So, with his star rapidly waning, and his finances almost exhausted, Campbell returned to Coniston for a 300mph dash on 4th January 1967. It ended in a disastrous back-somersault, and the great hero of thousands of schoolboys sank below the waves without trace; his body never to be seen again. Our school class watched as it happened and, even among the tough instructors who were leading us on our outward bound course, there wasn't a dry eye.'

The Campbell speed story began with the breaking of the world land speed record by Malcolm Campbell at Pendine Sands (Wales) in 1924, when his Sunbeam Bluebird achieved 146.163 mph. In 1937-9 he took four world water speed records in Bluebird K3. By 1955 it was his son Donald who began to collect a series of seven water speed records with the jet powered Bluebird K7. The upper view is a signed photo of Campbell racing Bluebird K7 down Ullswater, whilst the lower view shows him coming ashore at Glenridding. GRC

THE ULLSWATER STEAMERS

The steamer Raven leaving Howtown for Glenridding

To boldly go where no man has gone before, might once have been an appropriate aphorism for Ullswater, for in years past the top of the lake was really remote. Even in recent times it was hard to get to unless you happened to have your own boat or a horse that was brave enough to tackle the dangerous rocky paths over Stybarrow Crag. The alternate route ran along the east and north sides of the lake, but then one had to cross over Boredale and cut over the shoulder of land between Place Fell and Angle Tarn Pikes before descending the steeply sided hill to Patterdale.

However, on a miserably wet summer afternoon in 1859, all that changed when the first Ullswater steam boat, a vessel called the *Enterprise* made its maiden voyage. It was an era when public demand for travel on the lakes was growing and, incidentally, the same year that Coniston Water's famous *Gondola* also made her debut.

The arrival of the *Enterprise* had been anticipated for several weeks, and the *Carlisle Patriot* newspaper described the events as 'the chief topic of conversation in the district'. The 'Local Intelligence' column on 21st May 1859 revealed that the name of the 80 foot iron-built paddle steamer was still not known, or at least if it had been decided it had not been made known to the general public.

Rumour suggested that she would be called the *Dalemain* in

honour of the well-respected lord of the manor, but when launch-day came, seemingly on 16th July, the name *Enterprise* was finally made public. The weeks before launch-day were very busy indeed. At what the paper called the Ullsmere boat-house, which was near the site of the present Pooley Bridge pier, the *Enterprise* (built by the Liverpool-based firm of H. M. Lawrence & Co.) was being assembled having been delivered to the lake in sections.

The *Enterprise,* unlike its star-trekking counterpart did not have warp speed and its engine was rated at a mere 16-horsepower. It was, however, described as 'a luxurious paddle steamer with both ladies and gentlemens saloons.' Each of these saloons was around 20 feet in length, with adjoining wash rooms and other facilities.

Luxurious as she was however, her landing points still left much to be desired. The Ullswater Steam Navigation Company had been deadlocked in their negotiations with local landowners in the weeks prior to the steamer's arrival, so they had only just started work on the new landings. This work was still in progress when the passenger services began and a 90 feet long quay was in the process of being built on the Pooley Bridge side of the boat house.

The jetty at Howtown Bay was also being prepared, but those

planned near Lyulph's Tower and Aira Point did not materialise. At the south end a jetty was however being built near Patterdale by Mr W. H. Askew (a keen supporter of the company), on his own property. A provisional launch date of 20th June was mentioned in the local newspaper, but the work on the *Enterprise* was so detailed that the event had to be put back by almost a month.

As the big day drew closer, with the fitting of the boiler and other engine parts going very well indeed, negotiations were taking place between the steamer company and carriage owners who could set up a connecting service with the boats. The proprietor of the Sun Hotel in Pooley Bridge, a Mr Brownrigg, was the first to oblige with his horse-drawn omnibus between the village and Penrith and back, something he offered to do three times a day.

It seems that directors of the London & North Western Railway were also happy to help, by building a summer-only halt on their main London - Scotland line at Yanwath. However, as this was just under 2 miles south of Penrith, it was later decided to improve connections from the main station as it was very shortly to become a major junction with lines heading north, south, east and west.

The launch of *Enterprise* and its subsequent trials seemed to go off without a hitch, so the date of the first passenger service was arranged for Saturday, 13th August 1859. The 'hand-over' ceremony, in which the new craft was officially transferred to the Ullswater company directors, took place at 11 o'clock that morning. Then there was a nervous wait for everyone there, including a whole host of people who were to be the *Enterprise* 's first-passengers.

Unfortunately, although the vessel was already in steam, and looking ready to depart, a series of niggling delays led to the directors having a long and serious talk with the contractors. Much of this delay was caused by teething problems of one sort or another and also due to the apparent inexperience among the Ullswater company's staff. At one point it even looked likely that the steamer would stay in port, which would have been more than a little embarrassing for her new owners! Eventually, with the weather starting to worsen, the contractor Mr Lawrence decided to be 'steersman' for the big occasion. He got himself ready and then gave the 'nod' to the company directors, who in turn welcomed the passengers aboard at last.

Just as the maiden voyage began, the rain started, quite light at first but before long it was lashing it down. The passengers had to rush reluctantly for the twin saloons and put up with watching the scenery go by through rain-streaked windows or port-holes. To relieve the boredom of being stuck inside the cabins during the hour-long journey to the top end of the lake, two of the passengers were asked to sing and play a cornet or violin to entertain the others. A few passengers did brave the rain for a better look at the fells but they soon had second thoughts, quickly going below once again and only re-emerging when the far end of the lake was finally reached.

However when the *Enterprise* prepared to dock, there was quite

Pictures of Lady of The Lake *in steam days are quite hard to find, and the bulk of the 'known' views tend to feature* Raven. *This situation will undoubtedly and inevitably change after this book is published. So may we make an appeal for assistance in finding pictures of* Lady *in her earlier period on the lake, and if any one can assist they are requested to contact the publishers or the steamer company at their Glenridding office. This undated view of the* Lady *shows her in steam days, at the Patterdale pier. This pier was a little further along the lake than the present pier, which was actually built on 'new' land created by debris washed down by the Kepple Cove disaster of 1927.* CG

ABOVE: *Seen in July 1911, the SY* Raven *waits at Pooley Bridge landing stage. The vessel was 112 feet long, had a 15 feet beam and a displacement of 100 tons.* CG

BELOW: *The open steering position of the vessel was eventually replaced with a wooden wheelhouse which had been taken from a redundant trawler. This view is taken near Silver Point about 1934, in what was probably the last season before its 110hp non-condensing steam engines were replaced by two 8-cylinder National Gas & Oil Engine Co. power units.* CG

a commotion on the deck and jetty. A steward on the boat had thrown a rope from the boat to enable her to tie-up to one of the jetty posts but the man who caught the rope thought he could stop the steamer on his own and pull her right up to the pier. Some of the passengers laughed as the steward remonstrated with the rope-catcher, but then the rope caught him, dragging him by his ankles and flipping him upside-down on the spot. Another young man, standing on the quayside near where the boat's paddle wheel was still turning, suddenly had the rope across his face and he was pinned against the craft in what he protested afterwards was 'anything but a comfortable position'.

The passengers weren't laughing after the severity of the situation was realised, but everyone was thankful that no one was injured. When the excitement ended the passengers disembarked to explore the village but most either boarded the omnibus laid on by the landlord of the White Lion Inn or simply ran there to get out of the rain.

After an hour's stop (which by rights should have been spent basking in the sun at the lakeside or having a picnic and enjoying what was actually a red-hot drought-hit summer) the passengers returned and boarded the *Enterprise* for the trip back to Pooley Bridge. Perversely, as the passengers finally alighted from the boat, the dark clouds dispersed to herald a lovely, clear evening!

The *Carlisle Patriot* commented on the maiden journey stating that the *Enterprise* was: 'a commodious vessel with cabin accommodation of a superior quality. She sails swiftly and steadily, although the arrangements for landing passengers and the discipline of the crew are not yet quite complete; yet in the course of a little time, and with the experience of two or three more trips, her little defects may be remedied and there can be no doubt that she will prove another great source of attraction to this beautiful locality.' The crew did get better it seems, for after the teething troubles were overcome, she seems to have sailed her cruises with great success up to 1876.

On Wednesday, 20th June, 1877, a large number of people gathered along the shoreline to watch the launch of the lake's second steamer. The new boat was originally going to be called *Penrith Castle*, but its owners decided it would be more fitting to call her *Lady of The Lake*. She was designed by Mr Douglas Hebson, of Penrith, and built by Seath's of Glasgow who also transported her to Ullswater in sections. Miss Williamson of Fermilee performed the launching ceremony.

The local paper reported 'the handsome new screw steamer weighing 60 tons and carrying 115 tons register slid perfectly into Ullswater.' The column continued 'the *Lady of The Lake*, which measures 97 feet, was soon scheduled on the Pooley Bridge-Patterdale run at an average of twelve knots (13 miles) an hour. For the time the *Lady of The Lake* will be the only Ullswater steamer in action as the *Enterprise,* which had been put on extra duties the previous Autumn is not presently available.' Just 4 years after this debut, *Lady* sank at her moorings in 1881. She was soon pumped out by divers, re-floated and according to the local paper 'made ship-shape and Bristol fashion', and the programme of summer sailings was saved. (The same thing actually occurred again during a storm in 1958).

Breakdowns and availability problems showed the folly in relying on just one vessel. This led the company to invest in another vessel, for by this time the *Enterprise* is reported as 'having come to grief' although another account says it had been sold. Whatever the fate of the *Enterprise* it was intended to purchase the steamer *Wyvern*, but this idea failed after it sank in Windermere on 24th February 1876 just before its planned transfer to Ullswater.

Sadly, in January 1966, Ullswater *was* reduced to just a single steamer, the *Raven*, after a disastrous fire broke out when the *Lady* was laid up for the winter. This put the steamer out of action for 13 years, but the boat was salvaged, fully rebuilt and put back into service in 1979. Today, approaching her 125th birthday, she still forms part of the regular service.

The second boat built on Ullswater was the *Raven*, which was named after Ravencragg, the home of company director W H Parkin. It cost £2,650 to build (around £225,000 in modern terms) and was delivered in sections by rail and steam wagon from the works of Seath & Co. in Rutherglen (Glasgow), a firm who also built the Windermere steamers *Lady of The Lake* and *White Swan*. Her designer was once again Mr. Hebson, who had now moved to Ullswater from Penrith.

Work began in April 1889 as the *Raven* was assembled at the boathouse near Pooley Bridge. The launch was made into a public celebration, when Miss Winifred Parkin, performed the ceremony on 11th July 1889. In fact that Thursday turned out to be the maiden voyage as well, and those who had anything to do with the new steamer (which was already in steam) were invited to climb aboard prior to the launch, .

When the whistle blew Miss Parkin struck out with the bottle to name the steamer, and the wedges were knocked clear of the slipway to allow the *Raven* to slide stern first into the Lake. The first journey with her small band of passengers began with great cheers as she settled gently on the water. With a great many onlookers now assembled at the shore, the *Raven* went on a short tour of the Lake. After returning to the boathouse the general public were allowed aboard to marvel at her, both inside and out, and they were impressed at what they saw. The steel-built vessel still had to get her carriage certificate, but once that was granted she entered service. Carrying up to 400 passengers at a time, she travelled the Lake at between 12 and 14mph (20-23 Km/h) courtesy of her 150-200 horsepower engine.

In August 1895 the *Raven* gained the distinction of becoming a temporary 'royal yacht' during the German Kaiser's visit to

ABOVE: *The steamer* Wyvern, *was destined for Ullswater in 1876 but sank before the transfer was achieved. The* Raven *was thus ordered as the second vessel, and she is seen here arriving at Howtown Pier early in her career on the lake.* CG

BELOW: *Smaller steam-powered vessels also plied Ullswater and one such vessel was the launch* Dolly *which later sank in the lake. It was eventually salvaged and restored to a pristine condition at the Windermere Steam Boat Museum, and thus forms a valuable part of Lakeland's nautical heritage. Yet it is the two steamers that still serve the lake that have done so much in this regard. Here* Raven *sails past Kail Pot Crag c1900.* CG

Lowther Castle from where he toured the area. For this event, even the landing stage got the red-carpet treatment. In their early years the present Ullswater boats really were steamers, but progress started to catch them up at the start of the 1934 season when the *Raven* was fitted with two 80hp diesel engines - although the distinctive funnel was retained for ventilation and historical purposes. The *Lady of The Lake* was converted two years later to an oil-burning system, but even so the name steamers has stuck down till today. The picture inset shows the two vessels at Pooley Bridge pier after their conversion, it is taken from a postcard dated 1946, but probably pre-dates World War II.

Seasons tend to last from Easter to the end of October, and the reliability of the service is very high. The full service links Pooley Bridge pier, a mile from the village, to Glenridding Pier via Howtown jetty, to cater for Howtown, Sandwick and Martindale.

In fact, when the service was introduced in 1859, the company made a point of linking the ferries with horse-drawn coaches from Penrith to Pooley Bridge in order to reduce the waiting times for their passengers. At the end of the 1950s, plans were finally made to establish a small landing stage where the Aira Beck enters the lake. However, the trial plan to allow the passengers to head straight for the nearby beauty spot was not a commercial success and thus short-lived.

In April 1906, the first experiments in motor travel linking Penrith to Pooley Bridge and Ullswater were started, after an agreement between the ferry providers and the Penrith and District Road Carrying Company, but the bus service was not always as reliable as it should have been.

Today a much more reliable bus service is operated by Cumberland Motor Services from Penrith to Glenridding, whilst a Royal Mail post bus links Penrith and Howtown. Both of these services call at Pooley Bridge for those wanting a lake cruise, and in the height of summer a service links Ullswater and Windermere, so there is the chance to sail on both lakes. The steamers offer the most relaxing way to explore Ullswater, and connected with good bus links one can easily leave the car behind for the day.

Back in 1954 there were proposals to withdraw the vessels altogether but whilst that never happened, the fire on *Lady of The Lake* caused such extensive damage that few thought that this steamer would ever re-enter service. Yet on 19th May 1979 around 130 people watched as the (then) Home Secretary William Whitelaw, and Lord Wakefield (the owner), 'relaunched' the *Lady* after her £55,000 restoration. Before entering full time service she spent two days 'on contract' to a television film unit who were making a 'TV drama' about an injured Rugby League player.

Naturally, not everything has been plain sailing, and the steamers have had their minor troubles, but these vessels have safely plied the waters of Ullswater year upon year. In order to maintain this fine record each winter both boats are taken out of Ullswater by the slipway at Waterside Farm. Here they are routinely overhauled and made ready for next season. Then, before re-entering service, the vessels are both subject to annual safety inspection by the Department Of Transport.

Not only have the vessels' owners, played a very important part in preserving this unique piece of Lakeland history, they are also concerned in playing their part in conserving the countryside around the lake. In March 1998, the company instigated an initiative to support the Lake District National Park Authority in their effort to raise funds to maintain the path from Howtown to Patterdale (one of the best walks in the Ullswater area).

The then Chief Executive of the company, Mr. R.A.M. Coyne, added 10 pence to the price of single tickets for trips between Glenridding and Howtown, and all this extra cash has been handed over to the Authority so that they could maintain the path which the author Alfred Wainwright once called the loveliest lakeshore walk in the entire Lake District. The LDNPA area manager Peter Davies praised the idea, and said it would 'genuinely help' - for around 50,000 people are reckoned to annually walk between the piers at Howtown and Glenridding, or vice-versa.

Details of sailing times can be obtained from:
The Ullswater Transit & Navigation Co,
13, Maude St. Kendal;   *Tel: 01539 721626.or*
The Pier House, Glenridding; Tel: 017684 82229

The Ullswater Post Bus service at Glenridding c1912 with an Albion motor coach; note the curtains to keep out the wind and rain. GH

With the comparative ease of access that travellers enjoy today, we may tend to forget how isolated the Ullswater area was until the coming of mechanised transport in the 19th-century. However, evidence of the old 'coaching' days are still to be found on most larger-scale maps where you may trace the route of the Old Coach Road between Dockray and the quarries at Threlkeld, near Keswick, and the moorland route by way of Barbary Rigg and Hause Well.

Although horse-drawn buses and coaches had taken visitors down to the lakeside for many years, it was not until the heyday of the railway-building era of the mid-1800s that the start of mass tourism began. By then the levels of optimism and confidence in this new method of transport were so high that nothing seemed able to get in its way, including seemingly impossible mountain routes. No longer were railways content to confine themselves to industrial areas, and even remote areas like Cumberland and Westmorland were opened up.

There was some level of opposition however, with anti-rail opponents including Wordsworth who battled against the lines planned to penetrate the Lake District. Yet their protests were to little avail, and by the mid-1840s even the great obstacle of Shap summit was being assailed by the Lancaster & Carlisle Railway. It provided a branch to Kendal and Windermere and reached Penrith in December 1846.

It thus became the gateway to the northern lakes and with the growing numbers of passengers, facilities were upgraded at Penrith station in the 1860s, around the same time as routes were opened westward to Keswick and Workington and to Appleby and Darlington in the east, although none of these lines ever reached Ullswater. As the lake lay in a bowl amidst surrounding hills and it would have only required a few miles of track from Penrith, so many viewed the construction of a railway branch line to Pooley Bridge as a mere formality.

The clamour of tourists eagerly wanting to see more of Ullswater by the mid-19th century was really the start of the pressures that would eventually explode on the Lake District. At that time only horse-drawn charabancs and stagecoaches were available to provide a link from Penrith (although some of these services actually ran to Newcastle via Alston in the summer). Many simply walked from the station to Ullswater, although some enterprising farmers were able to provide transport down to the lake on their return from Penrith market.

Quite why the branch line proposals failed is not known, but this may have been partially due to the opposition people like Wordsworth had shown to the Windermere line. Yet it is ironic that the railways were being opposed by the romantic poets who had done so much to bring the beauty of Lakeland to the public's attention, thus stimulating the influx of visitors.

ABOVE: *Pictured at the head of Kirkstone Pass, Mr. Thornycroft's motor bus stands with its open top deck, solid tyres and acetylene lights; none of which were really suitable touring Lakeland's mountain passes.*

BELOW: *This undated view shows a Cumberland Motor Services TS8 with a Massey body (of 1938 vintage) as it runs on what were then the quiet roads alongside Ullswater.* JS/VP

Another stagecoach service started from Langwathby to Penrith and Ullswater, in conjunction with the opening of the Settle and Carlisle (Midland) Railway as from May 1876. It arrived at Ullswater in time to connect with the steamboat service, thus giving day visitors the opportunity to either explore the lake or wander round Pooley Bridge. But what was really needed to cater for the masses wanting to travel, was a direct rail link to the steamer pier at Pooley Bridge. On these proposals, the *History of Penrith* in 1894 quotes.

'Still another scheme was put before the public, on the completion of the Midland extension from Settle to Carlisle, when it was considered necessary, (if the town of Penrith was to maintain its position as the best market town in the north), that a connecting line between the town and some point of the Midland system, at Langwathby or Lazonby, was felt necessary to bring farmers and villagers from the Eden Valley and east fell-sides to the market, but this has not yet been accomplished, although it had tacked on to it another little scheme of tapping the Lake District at Pooley.' This flowery quote shows the grand hopes that a branch line would be built from the Settle-Carlisle route, which (in turn) provided communications with the West Riding of Yorkshire and the Midlands, by means of a route through the Pennines.

Just how those who wished to protect the lakes would have received such a plan is another matter. For example we might record the way that Wordsworth reacted to the news of the Windermere branch line when it had opened 30 years before, and to say he was not pleased with the scheme would be an understatement. He despised the railways and felt they were bringing in too many people, and to him that meant the Lake District would be spoiled forever! Others also held his views.

Although the Midland's Ullswater route was never built (due to the company's high expenditure commitments elsewhere) local railway campaigners took heart from the Light Railways Act of 1896, which allowed rural branch lines to be built to less costly specifications. In the spring of 1897 a scheme was suggested for a Penrith to Pooley Bridge line, quoting passengers (for the steamers), agricultural produce and lead traffic as its principal sources of revenue. When this idea failed, other schemes were devised to take its place.

There were also plans for cargo vessels to link the proposed railhead with Patterdale, in order to serve the busy lead mines around the head of the valley. Unfortunately none of the schemes ever materialised, nor did the Mid-Cumberland Light Railway plan which offered to link the area around Troutbeck and Penruddock with north-west Cumbria. It was therefore left to a horse-drawn charabanc service that was implemented to serve the post offices on the route between Crook-a-Beck in Patterdale and the main office in Penrith. It ran on Tuesdays, Thursdays and Saturdays, providing a service for both tourists and local passengers.

However horse-drawn transport was insufficient for the large numbers wanting to travel, and the Victorian era demanded mechanisation. Yet it was not until 1906 that a motorised bus service began, when a new company tried a bold experiment under the title of Penrith Motor Services Ltd.

They purchased a fleet of three brand new 35-hp buses, and each of these had a seating capacity for 16. This capacity could be extended to 24 if the 'convertible' body was lifted off to leave an open-topped charabanc. Despite their early date these buses were of a forward-thinking design, with features that some modern coaches could almost be proud of. Eighteen feet long, they had back doors with special access steps for the elderly or 'infirm', whilst the all-round windows had glass panels that could be removed for a better view of Ullswater.

One of the new vehicles was put on trial on a Thursday morning in April 1906, taking a dozen passengers and ten hundredweight of wire to represent a full load. A consultant engineer from the Automobile Club attended trials of the bus on a series of routes in Penrith, before going on to the more-challenging hilly, twisting lanes around Penruddock near Ullswater. After the trials an agreement was signed with the steamer company, to provide a connecting service between their vessels and Penrith. The passengers were impressed at the outset, but a series of 'breakdowns' meant that the horses were still needed. In time, reliability improved and as the first decade of the 20th Century came to an end, motor-charabancs were doing a roaring 'tour' trade. Towards the end of that decade, the motor engineer Tom Thornycroft had also helped to introduce an open topped double-deck tour bus service in the Lakes, and it frequently ran into the Ullswater valley. One fine picture shows this bus at the head of Kirkstone Pass, but you can only imagine how nerve-wracking it would be to travel down towards Patterdale on the front upstairs seats!

Yet it was the tourist traffic that spurred on the development of local services. Despite the advent of World War I, by 1915 a post-bus service was running between Penrith and Patterdale. Despite various wartime restrictions it served the area reasonably well, but the days of the small operator were already numbered. In due course, notably during the depressed years of the 1920s, the Ribble Bus Company from Lancashire began taking over the local firms, most notably the Lancashire & Westmorland Motor Services in 1927. The other company to develop routes in the area was the Cumberland Motor Services. After the Second World War there was a huge increase in holiday bookings all over Britain, both by rail and coach and the Lakes experienced a great deal of pressure on the narrow winding lanes. The coming of the 1940s and '50s saw the wide-spread development of the tour bus market, something which exploded when the M6 motorway finally opened in the 1970s. All of this impacted on roads that were, and still are, far from up to the job!

ABOVE: *Passing the nameboard PENRITH FOR ULLSWATER LAKE, a London Midland & Scottish railway 4-6-0 No.10899 pulls into Penrith in the early 1930s.* AE

BELOW: *Awaiting a working to Keswick and Workington via the North Lakes in July 1958, Ivatt Class 2MT 2-6-0 No.46488 stands in Penrith (For Ullswater) Station.* TW

Public Transport Today!

The 1990s have seen an increase in public transport services to (or around Ullswater) as people seek 'greener' and more relaxing ways to travel around the Lake District. As more and more people begin to appreciate the need to reduce the amount of car journeys being made in the Lake District, it is important to point out that alternatives are now becoming more readily available. As the new millennium dawns, a greater effort is being made by the local authorities and transport providers to balance the economies of public service in a rural area with the expectations of those who wish to explore the region. With initiatives like Local Agenda 21 starting to play a role in influencing good public transport provision, the future possibilities for reducing traffic on Lakeland's roads promises to be quite exciting. Few readers will disagree with the notion that it is much nicer to let someone else take the strain of driving, providing (of course) that there is a good public transport service at affordable costs.

As far as Ullswater is concerned, at the time of writing, there **are** several viable alternatives to the private car. For example, the 'Patterdale Rambler' bus services now runs a regular service between Penrith, Pooley Bridge and Patterdale, every day in summer and Mondays - Saturdays in winter. Double-deck buses offer superb top-deck views, never seen by motorists. The 'Kirkstone Rambler' from Ambleside to Patterdale is going from strength to strength and there are now direct summer bus services from Keswick to Patterdale. For a taste of real Cumbrian life, a trip on the Matterdale Post bus is an unforgettable experience, as you travel with the postie through the narrow lanes of the quieter eastern side of the lake. Combining buses, lake steamers and walks can provide memorable days out, giving you a chance to see the lake from every angle, and providing excellent opportunities for linear walks with no need to return to a parked car.

One popular trip is to take the ferry from Pooley Bridge to Howtown, walk along the lakeshore to Patterdale and then catch the bus back. Alternatively you could catch the Post bus to Martindale and back to Howtown, before catching the boat. If you want a circular tour seeing a wide variety of scenery catch the 'Patterdale Rambler' to Patterdale, then change to the 'Kirkstone Rambler' for the exhilarating journey over the pass to Ambleside. After spending some time in Ambleside you can take the 555 bus back to Keswick and then the X5 back across to Penrith. Cumbria County Council and the Lake District National Park Authority are both working together to improve public transport services in the Lake District. From the summer of 1998 they introduced improvements to the 'Patterdale Rambler' Sunday service, with a bus running right through from Carlisle.

These are just a few ideas, but why not contact the **Journey Planner Enquiry Line** number for further help in planning your day out. The authorities are also working to improve information about public transport, to help people discover Ullswater in an environmentally sustainable way. Timetables, including the comprehensive timetable booklet *Getting Around Cumbria and the Lake District* are available from Tourist Information Centres. To order timetables or for information on all bus, rail and boat services within Cumbria phone: The Journey Planner Enquiry Line on **01228 606000**, or:-

visit the Journey Planner Website at www.cumbria.gov.uk or write to Citadel Chambers, Carlisle, Cumbria, CA3 8SG.

But wherever possible, **please leave the car behind**, and support these worthwhile initiatives to provide a really user-friendly public transport system and help protect Ullswater for future generations. At a time when 91% of travel through the Lake District is made by private car, **all of us** should consider the use of alternative methods of transport!

With an advertising slogan 'Whatever You Want, Where Ever You Are', this local bus could almost be advertising the area around Ullswater and not Yellow Pages. Seen in Pooley Bridge, this Bristol double-decker is working Cumberland Motor Service's Patterdale - Penrith route. AE

HELVELLYN

The Helvellyn range, which is climbed more often than any other Lakeland fell today. RK

At 3,116 feet (950 metres) above sea level, Helvellyn is the second highest mountain in the Lake District, beaten only in its altitude by Scafell Pike (3,206 ft). Helvellyn is part of a large plateau, and a cluster of fells make up the range including Low Man, Raise, White Side, Nethermost Pike, Catstye Cam and the intriguingly named Dollywaggon Pike. The plateau reaches a height of well over 3,000 feet above sea level and stretches from Grisedale Tarn in the south to Threlkeld Common in the north. It is about 9 miles (14.5km) long and about 4.3 miles (7km) across at the widest point, and consequently forms the most extensive area of high fell country in the Lake District.

It is also distinctive because of its many glacial features; troughs are represented by Grisedale Tarn, cirques (bowl-shaped hollows known locally as coves) are found at Red Tarn and Nethermost Cove, and aretes (sharp ridges) are seen in the precipitous crests of Swirral Edge and Striding Edge.

The meaning behind the name Helvellyn has formed great debate, but its origin is most probably Cymric and it may mean yellow mountain, or mountain down which a yellow river falls. As the Cymric word lyn or lin meant a waterfall, so the use of the term 'Hevel-lyn' may give substance to the idea.

The view of Helvellyn from the south side is surely the best of all, and from this direction the mountain was climbed many times by the poet William Wordsworth. He first began his exploration as a youth, but later climbed the summit in the company of other notable characters of his period. For example, in 1805 he was accompanied on one climb by the poet Samuel Taylor Coleridge and Humphrey Davy, the inventor of the miner's safety lamp. The artist Benjamin Haydon even got Wordsworth to 'pose' for a portrait on the fell in 1840, when the poet was in his 70th year.

In April that same year an artist called Charles Gough came to grief on the mountain, falling while walking above Red Tarn. In all it would be some three months before his body was found but his sole companion, a little terrier, somehow made her way down the mountain side to reach her master's body. Here she faithfully waited by his side, but by the time they were found the dog had given birth to a litter of puppies! This event inspired many stories and poems, including ones by Wordsworth and Sir Walter Scott. To commemorate this feat of loyalty, a plaque was erected at the point from which it was supposed that the unfortunate Gough fell.

Aviators Bert Hinkler and John Leeming found an even harder way to reach the summit on Wednesday 22nd December 1926 when they landed an aeroplane on the precarious plateau. The intrepid duo took off from Lancaster, but a bout of engine trouble compelled them to make a forced landing at the childrens' orthopaedic hospital at Calgarth Park, Windermere. Whilst the children revelled in the excitement of having this wonderful machine (registered G-EBPH) on their lawn, for two hours the aviators tried to sort out the misfiring engine. After refuelling they finally took off once again, with John Leeming shouting to the nurses and the kids: 'We shall be on the top of Helvellyn in ten minutes' - and they were! Bert Hinkler skillfully landed the 'plane ten yards from the summit and just thirty yards from the precipice of Striding Edge.

They could see the artist's monument on the summit, but tried not to read it, before they set off over the 750 feet (229m) precipice above Red Tarn in a sensational and daring act. It could easily have ended in disaster as they plunged earthward for a few hundred feet, but their craft levelled out with a deafening roar as its propeller beat against thin air, lifting it away and out of danger. In time, another monument was built on the summit, celebrating the marvellous feat by Hinkler and Leeming.

The fact that Helvellyn was such a dangerous place prompted many visitors to secure the services of a guide, and one of the most famous was a tailor by the name of Johnson Thompson. Although Johnson was actually a Grasmere Guide, he had climbed Helvellyn something like 1,200 times before his death on 28th February 1925 at the age of 74. He first came to prominence by winning the tough Helvellyn fell race as a 27-year-old in 1878. He went on to earn more respect by leading sunrise treks up Helvellyn, after which he would return back to base to collect a daytime party and it was not unknown for him to do sunset trips as well - thus often doing three or even more trips a day!

His experience and dedication were rewarded at the age of 72, when he was commissioned to lead members of the Dutch Royal family to the summit. His party included Queen Wilhelmina, her Consort Prince Henry, and their daughter the Crown Princess Juliana. The family were staying at Rydal Hall, near Grasmere, and Thompson acted as their guide for walks to Helvellyn and Fairfield in June 1923. Afterwards Princess Juliana sent him a postcard (with a picture of the Royal Dutch Palace at Het Loo) thanking him for a lovely holiday.

RIGHT: *Today the summit is busy with walkers, and occasionally used by rescue helicopters when walkers fail to take the mountain seriously. Yet, all those who attain its lofty heights will not fail to be inspired by the majesty of the place or be in awe of the many events that have taken place here.* RK

KIRKSTONE PASS & BROTHERS WATER

To the southeast of the Helvellyn range, and beyond Fairfield, a deeply grooved pass is found between Red Scree and Ravens Edge. For centuries it has been a crossing place for mankind, linking Ullswater with Windermere. In the days when stone-age man came to the lakes in search of sharp hard slates for use as implements such as axes and arrow heads, Kirkstone was a most convenient route. Indeed, with its supply of readily available materials, some historians believe that this was not only a trade route, but a source of the materials also. The modern name of Kirkstone originates from the mediæval period and is said to be taken from a huge stone that stands close to the 1,493 feet (455m) summit. Said by many people to look like a church, it bestows the name Kirk (church) stone.

It is supposed that a religious altar or shrine was placed on, or around this stone, where travellers could pay homage and give thanks to God for their safe journey. In the pre-Christian era it is almost certain that the druids had a similar use for the stone; so this is a little example of Christianity borrowing from the pagans!

Though it is nowhere near as steep as the Honister and Wrynose passes in the western part of the Lakes, it is still a challenge for modern motorists. At one time there were roads either side of the Kirkstone Beck, which cascades down from the summit towards Brothers Water, and these former 'bridleways' still exist. Today one forms the main A592 road but the one on the west side of the valley, exists only as a 'well-engineered' terrace now used as a footpath.

Where this path reaches the summit, there is a section of 'metalling' around 765 yards (700 metres) long, close to the foot of Red Screes, and parts of it are up to 21 feet (6.2 metres) in width. Some historians believe this to have been a Roman road, which once connected Whitbarrow near Penrith, to Troutbeck near Ambleside. The arguments that are used to back up this theory are recorded in the excellent book *Roads and Trackways in the Lake District*, by Brian Paul Hindle.

A pack-horse trail used the ancient route for many years, and the summit inn served this type of traffic for two hundred years before any major improvements were made. An early atlas, John Ogilvy's *Britannia* of 1675, shows the route and it appears on maps in Robert Morden's *Camden's Brittania* of 1695. By 1685 there was a definite road from Pooley (Bridge) that continued on to Ambleside, using Kirkstone Pass on the way. What we know as the A592 today began to take shape around 1840 when it was 'improved', but it was a long way from the present standards.

The heavy use of the pass made a mess of the gravel-based

Kirkstone Pass from Smithy Brow.

As the picture above shows, the route over Kirkstone was well used by horse-drawn coaches, but to descend the Pass in relative safety, the coachmen had to lock up one or both of the rear wheels with chains. This prevented the carriages from getting up too much momentum and becoming runaways. One of the operators was the hotel-owner Richard Rigg from Windermere. He very quickly realised he could capitalise on the sudden increase in visitor numbers due to the new railway link to Windermere, and in 1847 he began running excursions to many places in the Lake District. It was only a matter of time before Kirkstone and Ullswater were added to his list! GH

roads and something had to be done about the road as it was literally crumbling under the strain of the traffic. The matter was left until the Westmorland County Council was created in 1888, by which time it was so bad that the authority had to 'act with rapidity.' Accordingly gravel and other materials were laid in an attempt to form a solid and weatherproof track, but a decision was taken not to tar the surface.

Such engineering was however possible, for an experiment

into the use of tar and waste spar/quartz from the local mines, by John L. Macadam, had seen the substantial improvement of the mountain road over Hartside from Alston to Penrith in 1821. After the upgrade of the Kirkstone roads in 1889 a Hartsop man, Anthony Benson, was employed to maintain the highway, and his son Herd was appointed his Deputy. They were still there in 1903 when the Rector of Patterdale, the Rev. W P Morris, published his book *The Records of Patterdale*.

The pass had its share of important visitors too, and one of the most notable events was the Lakeland tour programme for the visit by the Germany Kaiser in 1895. Many people thronged Kirkstone just to see the royal party as it went over the pass that August. Due to the poor state of the road, the climb was still an arduous one for the cavalcade of horse-drawn carriages and it progressed at barely walking-speed. At least this allowed the Emperor extra time to admire the scenery, especially the impressive bulk of Helvellyn, and Ullswater far below, but a thoroughly modern problem was met at the summit - dozens of press photographers!

A feature of the pass is the inn, which has given succour to travellers since 1496 and was originally the Travellers' Rest. Today it is called the Kirkstone Pass Inn but it still provides food and lodgings, and its rooms with four-poster beds are located at 1,485 feet above sea level. As such it is the fourth-highest inn in Britain and it has long kept a visitors' book.

One of the entries in its pages for September 1898 tells the poignant tale of a pair of cycling friends from Manchester who were touring in the area with a tandem. After pushing it for much of the way up the south side of the pass, they called at the Inn for refreshments. They wrote their names and a message in the visitors' book before setting off again, bound for Patterdale and Ullswater. However, just over halfway down their brakes failed and they crashed at high speed. One of the cyclists, although shaken, was not badly injured but the other, a Mr Harry Moss, sadly suffered a fractured skull in the accident. He died of his injuries three days later, and a memorial plaque to him now marks the crash scene.

The Kirkstone route had seen many early motorists and cyclists coming to grief due to brake failure or other mishap on the long climbs, yet this very danger attracted others to 'beat the pass'. Despite the fact that the route was little more than a track strewn with gravel and loose stones, early motorists were soon challenging the terrain (and each other) in hill-climbs. The 'sport' took off with the 'Motor Trials' events before World War I, and it was in this kind of atmosphere that motoring really began to make its mark on the Lake District. These trialists found that the steep Lakeland passes like Kirkstone were perfect testing grounds for the vehicles, so they were included in the major runs in the first years of the century.

Following on from motor trials as early as 1900, an event that included Kirkstone Pass and Dunmail Rise was organised by the

Royal Automobile Club in 1908. This new motor reliability challenge covered 2,000 miles (3,219 km.) and was described at the time as 'probably the most ambitious to date.' It included many Lakeland roads, but it was at Patterdale that they gathered to face the fearsome might of Kirkstone Pass, although very few drivers had ever faced a challenge like this before. Kirkstone had been measured out for the contest, and the rough, dusty old track climbed at an average of 1-in-9 (12%) for 2 miles 523 yards. There was also a 'sting in its tail' with a 133-yard stretch at 1-in-6.75 (15%). Every stop on the road incurred a loss of points, so the drivers' aim was to go all out for the summit.

On Monday 27th June a grand total of 37 cars assembled at the foot of the pass just after lunch. Models of all varieties and sizes were there for the trial, but most of the smaller cars were beaten by the task. Even the more powerful cars had a hard time of things but they were all to be handicapped by the sharp turns and steep drops.

Despite excellent driving skills, a few came to grief in minor accidents, and most lost time with mechanical faults. A 6-hp De Dion failed the hill-climb test, but a 10-hp Cadillac slowly reached the summit successfully. Transmission problems just 50 yards from the summit brought a 20-hp Talbot to a halt, but its crew repaired the fault in less than 4 minutes and they completed their run.

Full marks for trying were given to the little De Dion that had three attempts at the climb before trying it in reverse. Even that attempt failed because of a carburettor problem, but finally the driver completed the run in the lowest forward gear. Another car to falter was an 8-hp Adler, but a 48-hp Rolls Royce, which had already tackled Dunmail Raise, showed the others how to take Kirkstone Pass in style.

A 25-hp car being driven by its creator, Mr. Tom Thornycroft,

came to grief when a rear tyre perished on the rough track, causing it to swerve and pile into a wall. The driver escaped virtually unscathed but his mechanic, Mr. Porter, received cuts to his face in the accident. Modern motorists have few of these problems, but the hill still takes victims, and a great many vehicle recoveries have to be effected here each year.

It is the winter that takes its more serious toll and the road is frequently closed to traffic. Some drivers recklessly ignore the closure notices, failing to understand that even though there might only be a modest snow fall in the valley, serious driving conditions could exist at the summit.

As you travel down towards Ullswater from Kirkstone Pass, you will not fail to notice the expanse of water that begins to appear as the valley widens out. It is obvious that this lake was once much larger than it is today, and evidence of the 'silting' process can be clearly seen.

With its reedy fringes, this pretty little lake is called Brothers Water, reputedly so named after two brothers died in a skating accident there long ago. The earliest known reference to this name is recorded as long ago as 1671 but it was also called the equally appropriate Broad Water in the late-eighteenth century.

Brother's Water. LE

However, the name may come from even older origins, and the scholarly opinion is that the name 'Brother' may be derived from the Old Norse name *Brothir,* and could thus date from as long ago as 1,500 years. The lake is best approached on foot by the lane leading from the attractive Brotherswater Inn, via a campsite near the lake. Brothers Water is probably best appreciated in the autumn, when the broad-leaf trees and the marsh reeds turn gold and yellow, but it is equally majestic in the deep of winter, especially when a full moon reflects upon its dark, still surface.

AROUND HARTSOP

Below Brothers Water lays a broad valley floor, which was obviously once part of the lake bed. The rich alluvial soil presents good pasture, even though it is well over 500 feet above sea level. Around these pastures, two major tributary valleys branch off from the Goldrill Beck. The first heads up through Hartsop, which is one of the most attractive little hamlets in the county. Its name literally means 'Valley of The Hart'; Hart being derived from the Old English 'Heorot' and 'hope' comes from the Low German (Saxon) 'opp' that means up, so the name literally means deer up.

ABOVE: *Hayeswater with the Straights of Riggindale beyond.* NT

Hartsop has always obtained its income from agriculture, but it was also once a centre for a thriving industry of textile manufacture and lead mining. Beyond here lay two beautiful valleys, Pasture Beck and Hayeswater Gill. In the mountains above are two small lakes which are well worth the walk to reach them. The first of these is Hayeswater which was once just a quiet tarn high up in the Lakeland fells, before it was damned in 1908. It used to be about half the size of Brothers Water (less than half a mile long and half that in width) and was at a height of around 1,367 feet (417m) above sea level. But all that good clean water was just what the nearby town of Penrith needed to avoid relying on the water it extracted from the River Eamont by means of a pumping engine.

An outbreak of enteric fever in 1891, forced Penrith's town council to seek a Parliamentary Bill for the scheme. Unlike the Mardale scheme that followed, only three people objected to the plan and it received Royal Assent in January 1907. The only real question was how much Hayeswater Tarn's owner, Lord Lonsdale, would be entitled to charge for the water. But he offered favourable terms and was rewarded by being asked to cut the first sod of the new pipeline in August 1908. This pipeline took an arduous route, going up the steep hillside to Hause Crag where a break-pressure tank was provided. From here it ran down Boredale, and went over Martindale Hause. The pipeline then climbed up on to Barton Fell, where another reservoir tank was installed. The dam of Hayeswater reservoir, measured 10 feet tall (3m) by 100 feet long (31m) and it was between 5 feet (2.6m) and 13 feet (4m) in thickness. Unlike the ugly dam at Thirlmere, it was made to blend in with the surrounding environment and look as natural as possible.

The other body of water to be found in the hills nearby is Angle Tarn, which is located between Hayeswater Gill and Bannerdale. Originally called Angilterne, it is said to have an old Norse name, Ongull, because of its 'fish-hook' shape. However it may also have connections with the Angles who once settled the area and bestowed the name Anglewood or Inglewood on lands north of Ullswater! The tarn has a small island (close to the eastern side), plus one or two other islets, and this surely makes it one of the best Cumbrian tarns as most do not have any islands. Nearby is the impressive landform of Heck Crag, which overlooks Bannerdale.

On the western side of the A592 are two more fascinating valleys, Dovedale and Deepdale, both of which have traces of early civilisation. Paths up these valleys are now well used by walkers, as they lead up to Fairfield 2,863 feet (873m) above sea level. Yet these tracks are of great antiquity, probably dating back to Celtic times. Both are very ancient trade routes, especially that through Deepdale which continued as a pack horse trail until the 19th century. Yet another route, and almost as old as that over Kirkstone, ran via the nearby Scandale Pass.

PATTERDALE

The village of Patterdale, with the unusual shaped White Lion Inn on the right.   AE

Patterdale Common and Grisedale cover a vast area at the south end of Ullswater. It is an area of rich geography and dramatic history, but all of this is missed by the motorist, who at best only senses the magnificence of it all. From the A592 at Grisedale Bridge you can see the attractive valley beyond, but only those who leave their cars behind will really get to know the land beyond. The path up the valley is virtually as straight as a dye for about three miles until it begins the climb to Grisedale Forest, before reaching Grisedale Tarn. This glacial lake nestles between Fairfield, Seat Sandal and Dollywaggon Pike, and it is the larger of the two tarns in the Helvellyn range. The fact that this valley has been used as a means of communication for many centuries is really quite obvious as you walk this way, especially when you cross the ridge and descend to Dunmail Raise, but what was the event that caused one boulder to become known as the Brother's Parting Stone?

The village of Patterdale is located on the Goldrill Beck, between its confluences with the Deepdale and Grisedale becks, and owes much of its existence to ancient commerce. For both of these valleys also carried important trade routes in times past as they connected Patterdale and Grasmere. It got its name from St. Patrick, who is believed to have walked to this serene valley just south of Ullswater.

This journey followed his shipwreck on the treacherous Duddon Sands, between Barrow-in-Furness and Millom in 540. Some may wonder how Patrick came to end up at the head of Ullswater, but having landed on the shores of south-west Cumbria, he would probably have found his way to one of the main trade routes. And as at least two of the routes from the coast came via Patterdale, it is not difficult to understand his reason for reaching here in due course. The missionary is well remembered in Patterdale and the local church (built in 1853) bears his name as does a well alongside the road to Glenridding. He was also commemorated in fine tapestries made by Ann Macbeth, who lived in Patterdale for 27 years until her death in 1948. One of her tapestries was given to Patterdale church and hung there for safekeeping after being praised by Queen Mary, the wife of King George V.

Patterdale is a collection of houses that evolved rather than being a 'planned' village, but this imparts its individual character. The school is an integral part of the community, and it is the centre of many of the social activities in the village although it has far fewer pupils now than it did 50 years ago. Some of the quaintest houses dated from the 16th century and were known collectively as 'The Township, but these were swept away by road improvements in the 1920s.

The White Lion in Patterdale is one of the Lake District's famous public houses, due to its unusual shape. The inn is of an indeterminate age, but it may date back to the late 18th century when the Mounsey family 'improved' the village. The Mounsey estate sold it to the Glasson Brewery Company in 1950, and today it provides one of the main focal points for locals and tourists alike. One frequent guest was William Wordsworth, who was in the pub when news of Nelson's death at Trafalgar was received in the village.

Patterdale is also well known for its 'Dog Day' sheep dog trials, usually held on the Saturday preceding the Bank Holiday Monday in late-August. The first Dog Day was held in 1901 and the event has grown from strength to strength. The Dog Day reflects Patterdale's main way of life, which is centred on hill farming. The farmers mainly breed Herdwicks and Swaledale sheep, both of which are perfect at surviving the harsh Lakeland winters, and farmers will tell you tales of their being dug out of snowdrifts after days or even weeks. These inhabitants of the fells sometimes embark on quite incredible journeys and it has been found that they can traverse 30 miles (48kms) of treacherous moorland to return to the fell where they were born, which can lead to problems (especially when they've been sold to another farmer)!

In the eighteenth century Patterdale was ruled by the so-called Kings of Patterdale, who lived in a house the locals called Mounsey's Palace, the forerunner of Patterdale Hall. The Mounsey's had become the landlords early in the 17th century and in 1648, a certain John Mounsey, together with his own 'army' had fended off a band of marauding Scots. This was the time of the Border Reivers, groups of lawless men who raided either side of the border with equal impunity. The Ullswater valley offered such thieves rich pickings, but on this occasion Mounsey's men ambushed them at the top of Stybarrow Crag. The challenge earned Mounsey great respect and relations between him and his tenants couldn't have been better.

RIGHT: *A really pastoral scene of the early 1950s, with a view of hay-making at Grizedale Bridge. With pitch-forks and hay rakes, the valuable fodder is gathered up for the long months of winter that lay ahead. The old horse-drawn hay cart has now been provided with a new form of motive power, a 40 year old Morris Cowley car. Devoid of its back end and cab, the vehicle has been converted and fitted with a new rear axle to form a cross between a pick-up truck and a tractor. GRC*

By the mid- to late-18th century another John Mounsey had gained a reputation for being miserly, and his tenants went through hard times as a result. The obituary, which appeared in *Gentleman's Magazine* in October 1793, was therefore very scathing of him. It read 'On the 21st September at Patterdale Hall on Ullswaterside, Westmorland, in his 92nd year of his age, John Mounsey, Esq., commonly called King of Patterdale, the owners of which place have since time immemorial been honoured with the appellation (name or title). John Mounsey was a sad miser and a most undesirable person who, with an income of £800 a year had the laudable ambition to keep his expenses down to £30 a year. This he was assumed to have done by heeling his socks with leather (to avoid buying shoes), sleeping in barns when not in his Palace, and wearing iron-shod clogs, but still expecting his tenants to keep him in clothes and food despite their poor means'.

Another John Mounsey rebuilt Patterdale Hall from scratch in 1796. He also made amends in the village, and rebuilt a number of houses making it 'a much more attractive place to live in.' Patterdale Hall was later sold to William Marshall, once MP for both Carlisle and East Cumberland. Much later it became a YMCA Hostel and also a hotel, although not before a major local controversy and a few lesser problems. In August 1934 the furnishings were auctioned following the death of Mr W. H. Marshall, and the well-attended three-day sale included 1,000 ounces (29kgs.) of Georgian and other silverware. Today the Patterdale Estate serves as a residential outdoor activity centre, and an important part of the local economy!

GLENRIDDING

View of Glenridding main street with a horse bus c1900, inset Glenridding a century later. GH.

Glenridding means the 'Glen overgrown with Bracken' and was derived from the Cymric words 'Glyn' and 'Rhedyn', but it had become Glenredyn by 1292. Today this is the main village in the area and is best known for its countryside activities, but its growth is entirely due to another reason as we will see.

There are many fine walks to undertake, some easy, some hard. Perhaps one of the loveliest, and certainly this writer's favourite, is the footpath to the summit of Keldas, with its impressive views over Glenridding, beyond which is the lovely Lanty's Tarn beauty spot situated high above Patterdale Hall. Another favourite route for many walkers is the track up the Glenridding Valley which is bordered by Birkhouse Moor to the south and Glenridding Dodd and Sheffield Pike to the north, all of which tower majestically over the village.

A walk up this valley will strongly make the point that the history of Glenridding is heavily connected with industry. For the very track you will use, makes a steady climb of about two miles up to the old Greenside Lead Mines. Long before the track was used by hikers and mountaineers, it was the way miners trod their weary way to and from work. It was also very well used by the horses and carts, steam waggons and motor lorries that brought lead down from the mines and smelt mill.

So, as you climb upwards to Greenside, you reach the unescapable fact that Glenridding can not be separated from the mines that once existed in these hills. Indeed this industry not only gave birth to the community, but it twice almost destroyed it. The greatest physical reminder of this industry are the huge spoil heaps above Greenside which will give some inclination of how extensively the area below ground was worked, whilst a permanent exhibition in the Glenridding information centre provides a visual record. Two very good books on the subject are also available locally, and we have given a brief over-view of the subject on page 61.

The spoil heaps may be very impressive, but beyond the mines lay more natural and scenic features including the Glenridding Screes that dominate much of the south flank of Sheffield Pike. More ambitious walkers, who are adequately equipped, can continue south west of the mines and reach one (or both) of the two imposing valleys below the summit of Helvellyn. These valleys are situated either side of the fell named Catstye Cam, and each has its own little lake; Red Tarn to the south of Catstye Cam and the remains of Kepple Cove Reservoir to the north of it. Wherever the walk leads to, there are good footpaths on either side of Glenridding.

The head of the lake, looking down to Patterdale and Glenridding. AE

Those less keen on walking can just sit and admire the scenery , especially looking over Ullswater towards Blowick. The shoreline at this end of the lake is really lovely and in their season snowdrops, daffodils, primroses and bluebells grow in profusion. The outlook here varies greatly, and it ranges from the massive, rugged bulk of Place Fell opposite Glenridding to the lush valley bottom where Goldrill Beck flows into the lake from Brothers Water.

Today's hustle and bustle contrasts greatly with life prior to the early-1900s. Before this Glenridding had been essentially isolated and unsophisticated, with lead mining being its main preoccupation. Others tended to get on with farming and there was little impact from tourism, until the mid-19th century when the steamers began plying the lake.

Although visitors did come, it was primarily an industrial working community. Limited accommodation and the poor road network created their own drawbacks, but the enterprising Thomas Cook's travel agency contrived to get people to this end of the lake by offering inclusive package tours that included rail tickets to Penrith, where trains were met by coaches that would in turn link with the lake steamers.

In November 1927 the village was devastated by a torrent of water that flowed from a 30 feet wide and 40 feet high breech in the Kepple Cove Dam. The Co-op, Walton's Store and the Millcrest Hotel were all badly damaged, and many valuable antiques were swept out of the hotel and lost forever. Although the village was covered in about a foot of mud and silt, the community quickly rallied round and with a great sense of spirit they soon got things back to normal. Eventually the mining company repaired the reservoir, but it was ruined financially by the huge compensation it had to pay. Then on the morning of Thursday, 20th August 1931 the dam failed again, but this time the damage was less severe. Mercifully no one was killed in either disaster, but after this second incident it was discovered that the bedrock on which the dam was constructed was either very shallow or non-existent, so it was finally abandoned. The mines would last only a further three decades, since when Glenridding has become ever more dependent on tourism to supplement agriculture. A legacy of the disaster is the land on the frontage of Glenridding, for the area where the steamer ferry car park is situated today was created on debris swept down the beck by the flood waters.

Along the A592 between Glenridding and Watermillock is one of the most attractive stretches of Ullswater, much of which is now in the care of the National Trust. Running between Glencoyne and Dobbin Wood, this stretch of land encompasses Glencoyne Park, Aira Force, the Aira Arboretum, Lyulph's Tower, Gowbarrow Park and Dobbin Wood. Ancient settlements have been found hereabouts, and an old causeway down through Glencoyne Park may indicate the existence of a Roman road.

It is a fact that pre-Roman settlers cleared the trees and cultivated both crops and livestock in the attractive location along the side of the lake, especially on the flat promontory of land that juts out into Ullswater near Glencoyne Bay. The Saxons and Vikings certainly settled here, and the very name Gowbarrow comes from the Norse word meaning windy hill. As we will reveal later, Lyulph's Tower was occupied around 1080 and not long afterward Gowbarrow Park became one of the 'forests' proclaimed by William the Conqueror's successor William Rufus (1087-1100).

By mediæval times both Gowbarrow and Glencoyne had been formed into one large hunting park, with walling erected to contain the red deer. A bailiff was employed to control the 'vermin', and he paid a bounty on the following animals: for killing a fox, 10 groats; a fox cub, 3 groats; an eagle, 3 groats; a pine marten, 3 groats; a wildcat, 2 groats and a raven, 1 groat. A groat was four pence (4d) in old money, or 1.667 new pence.

The estate also managed the lower fells as coppiced woodland, and the trees were cropped by rotation to supply wood for local needs. These included barrel making, bobbin manufacture, and charcoal burning. Even the bark was not wasted, as this was used to produce tannin. With regard to charcoal burning, whilst this was not as common as in the South Lakes, it was an industry that was carried out at some length in the woods around Ullswater. The end product was either used in the local ore-smelting industry or for the manufacture of gunpowder.

LEFT: *The spectacular Aira Force waterfall is one of the most famous natural features in the area and it takes its name from the Aira Beck and the Norse word foss (anglicised as Force) meaning waterfall. The deep ravine into which the beck falls has been formed at a point where the Skiddaw Slates meet the Borrowdale Volcanic Series of rocks. Years of erosion have now formed a spectacular gully through which the beck cascades, and where (on a sunny day) the light reflects on the spray to create the famous 'Aira Rainbow'. The prismatic effect of sunlight and water often creates a spectacular triple bow, and this feature continues to attract and amaze visitors.*

By the 1780s the Gowbarrow Estate had passed into the ownership of the Howard family from Greystoke, and the 11th Duke of Norfolk (Charles) began the restoration of the old Pele tower that had been used as a hunting lodge on the estate. He created the attractive Lyulph's Tower with a crenellated facade, which in the 1960s was used as the setting for a Cadbury's advert, where the hero descended the tower to enter a bedroom and leave a box of a famous brand of chocolates.

The actor in the feature was Gary Myers (doubled by stuntman Martin Grace), who was filmed jumping first from the Tower onto a passing lorry and then into Ullswater. The advert was filmed over three nights in November 1968 and to create the dramatic effects some 50 technicians were employed. As a result it became one of the most expensive adverts to film in the 13 years history of independent television in Britain to date. However, it was so well produced that it was still being shown well into the 1980s. And *all because the lady loved Milk Tray* after 15 years.

The Tower is however, a private home, and there is no public access to the building or its grounds. But it is not just for television that Lyulph's Tower has a claim to fame for it also has a great history and strong connections with Wordsworth who wrote about it frequently. Indeed, it is this part of Ullswater about which William wrote his famous poem *Daffodils*, after seeing the beautiful flowers growing on the mossy hillside above the lake.

Traditionally it is said that the tower got its name through Lyulph (or Liolf, or Ligwulf), the first owner of the lake. James Clarke's *Survey of The Lakes* (1787) comments that it was scarcely possible that the Lake had only had one owner, and it had surely got its name from another source. He said that it may have been named Wolfs' Water because the deep woods and almost-inaccessible mountains all around 'would undoubtedly afford a safe asylum to these animals'.

However, the man Lyulph is mentioned by old historians such as Speed, Guthrie and others, as having lived here at the time of the Norman Conquests. Their record says that Lyulph 'retired' here for a while. However, in 1080, he went to visit Walcher, Bishop of Durham, who paid him much favour. Jealous of this position, one of the Bishop's chaplains or kinsmen by the name of Gilbert killed Lyulph and the Bishop allowed him to escape. In respect for Lyulph, some of his supporters set out to extract revenge, and they killed the Bishop in front of his altar where he had gone for sanctuary.

In 1846 the Howard family planted an arboretum just below Aira Force, using several hundred specimens of trees with types brought from all over the world, including the Himalayan mountains. It is still there today, and forms an attractive feature of the estate which offers some splendid walks, all of which are detailed in a leaflet available from the National Trust. A tearoom (not managed by the Trust) is found in the car park and it provides adequate sustenance at the end of the most arduous of walks. The waterfall is around 60 feet. (18 metres) in height, and is topped off with a fine-looking stone bridge carrying a footpath from the A5091 road.

A few hundred yards upstream the Aira Beck features other falls including High Force, but this should not be confused with the mighty cascade of the same name that is found in Teesdale. The beck itself starts from the head of the remote Dowthwaite valley up on Watermillock Common, where Little Aira Beck meets Rush Gill. Aira Beck then heads loosely eastwards to the village of Dockray, where it is joined by Riddings Beck before it heads down to the lake.

The whole estate came up for sale at the start of the 20th-century, with the intention of selling off the land for housing. Such a desecration would have been unthinkable, but the 750 acres could command a high price due to the spectacular location of a relatively few prime plots. However £12,000 was raised for the purchase (around £823,00 in present day money) and the estate was officially handed to the National Trust in August 1906.

Since then the Trust have made progressive improvements, whilst maintaining the original qualities that made the estate so special. One of the most important provisions was a bridge at the top of Aira Force, which was built in the early-1930s as a tribute to local dignitary Sir Cecil Spring-Rice, from nearby Watermillock. Its construction made a splendid circular walk a possibility, and in the opinion of this author it is probably the second finest 'family walk' in the whole of the Ullswater Valley. It is just one of four walks that feature in the National Trust's local walk leaflet, but which ever option you choose you should walk to this bridge and look down the roaring cascade. The rainbow might be spectacular on a sunny day, but for me the best time to see the Force is after a prolonged period of heavy rain, especially when the autumn leaves are golden brown. In the quiet solitude stop and reflect on the beauty, and perhaps you will then understand why it so inspired Wordsworth!

TROUTBECK & MATTERDALE

Fell ponies grazing the hills above Matterdale. AE

Whilst the main visitor locations on Ullswater are Pooley Bridge, Patterdale, Glenridding, Aira Force, and Howtown, we should not forget that there are a host of small communities on the north side of the lake. Between Ullswater and the A66 there are a number of villages and hamlets, ranging from the remote and beautiful Dowthwaite to 'developed' Stainton in the east. Sadly we can only present a brief overview of these communities, but the good network of footpaths and minor roads will best enable you to explore them at your leisure.

Leading up from Ullswater the first village to be reached is Dockray, which boasts a very nice inn that caters for all needs. Personally I like Dockray, because it can be used as the starting point for many spectacular walks on Gowbarrow Fell or Matterdale Common. The two most rewarding are those leading to Dowthwaite, Birkett Fell and Hart Side 2,481 feet (756 metres) or the more strenuous walk to Great Dodd 2,807 feet (857 metres) and Stybarrow Dodd 2,756 feet (843 metres).

Further up the A5091 the traveller reaches Matterdale End village, surely best known for its ancient church, which was built in 1573. Designed by Lancelot Pattinson of Windermere, its outlook and setting must be one of the most commanding of any church in the region. The most significant of all the villages in this valley is the moorland settlement of Troutbeck, which may well seem to be little more than a sleepy hollow as the 20th century draws to a close.

Yet a hundred years ago, Troutbeck was one of the busiest villages in the area, for this was the railhead for Ullswater following the opening of the Cockermouth, Keswick & Penrith Railway to freight traffic in October 1864 (with passenger services beginning three months later). It served the needs of the farming community well, and an auction mart was established in fields alongside the station. Furthermore, the station also handled most of the lead traffic from Greenside.

The railway lasted until the evening of Saturday 4th March 1972 when a charter train ran from Penrith to Keswick with nearly 450 passengers aboard, all of whom wanted to say a final farewell. During that final journey there was a raffle in which one of the main Troutbeck station signs was won by a man from Penrith, whilst signs from other stations along the 18-mile (29kms.) route were also among the prizes. The railway officially closed the following Monday, but the tracks between Penrith and Flusco Quarry were left in place until mid-June 1972, because the Royal Train was due to use the line for an overnight stop. There are plans to revive the railway to Keswick now, but its closure in the first place was a ludicrous piece of stupidity that should never have been permitted. The prospect of using the railway for sustainable tourism should have been considered back then, but instead there was a mad dash to dispose of the line and use part of its track bed for road improvements. Perhaps the current proposals will lead to a re-awakening, and it may just be that Troutbeck station is not really dead, just gently sleeping!

Tranquil lanes and quaint buildings in Dockray. AE

DACRE & WATERMILLOCK

LEFT: *Dacre castle, now a private residence has a history dating back to Norman times, when a tower was constructed along the defensive line stretching from Richmond to Cockermouth. It was one of the important Border towers, and certainly one of the longest in active service. In due course it became part of the Huddleston Estate when Marie Hoton (a god-daughter of Queen Mary) married Andrew Huddleston of Millom Castle.*

To the east of Troutbeck stands an attractive conical-shaped hill named Great Mell Fell, the summit of which is 1,760 feet (537 metres) and has the site of an ancient Tumulus or burial mound. There is some debate over the history of this fell, but along with its nearby neighbour Little Mell Fell (1,657 feet - 505metres) it seems likely that it would have been used in British days as either a settlement or place of fortification. An earthworks dating from this period is also to be found in the valley between the two peaks, not far from Brownrigg. There may well have been some connection between these fells and the hill fort near Pooley Bridge, and in military terms the two hills would have been of great strategic value. Their name also carries with it a link with the Ancient British/Cymric period, as the name Mell comes from the word Meol which means bare.

The valley between these fells carries the pretty Dacre Beck which means 'trickling stream'. It has a distinct Ancient British history behind it as the celtic name for the beck is Dakru and is closely related to the Welsh root word deigr (flow of water) which is more commonly found in deigryn (teardrop). The Dacre then continues down to the small hamlets of Hutton and Hutton John, both of which take their name from the de Hoton family who held the fortified tower here in the reign of Edward I around 1282.

The village of Dacre had an important part in local history, and the Venerable Bede makes reference to a Saxon monastery at Dacore in 730. An ongoing series of archeological excavations has revealed many finds around Dacre, but the historians admit that there is still much more to discover about its past. Dacre Castle also had very ancient origins, and it was referred to as an old castle in the writings of William of Malmsbury back in 1131. He mentions it as the location for a congress when the Kings of Cumbria, England and Scotland met in 930. Its importance in the Saxon and British times can not be underestimated, and it is significant that this is the location of the Peace Of Dacre and Surrender of All England!

The next village on Ullswater-side is Watermillock, which also has very ancient origins. In 1215 the village was known as Wethermeloc, and in this its origins are shown for it literally means 'the little Hill where wethers (sheep) graze.' In addition to agriculture, the old industries around here included pencil making, snuff manufacture and charcoal production.

The area around Watermillock today contains some of the area's finest and most comfortable visitor facilities, in a clutch of grand old lakeside houses that have been converted into exceptionally fine country house hotels. Nearby is another attractive-looking country house called Hallsteads Manor, but this was destined to have a very different future than its neighbours. In August 1955 this building was converted into the Outward Bound Trust's new Mountain School. The venture was so successful that it had provided adventure days, holidays and training courses for well over 23,000 people in its first quarter-century. It still maintains this role today, providing specialised tuition in a range of activities, including mountain rescue. Because of its importance, the centre has attracted a number of famous visitors, including HRH Prince Charles.

One of the spectacular Ullswater winter sunsets, seen from Pooley Bridge. RK

Along with Glenridding, the most important settlement on Ullswater is the village of Pooley Bridge, which would have been settled very early in the history of the lake. Indeed, if the Celtic tribesmen who settled here had brought with them their traditional method of house building, this would have been one of the few parts of the lake in which they could have settled. When we say settled in the Lake, that is exactly what they did, for the Celts built their houses on wooden piles or posts elevated above a body of water. In the French Lake District, evidences of how the Celts lived in these 'stilt-house' dwellings has recently been uncovered by archaeologists.

At Lac Du Chalain in the Jura region of France (which is also connected to Arthurian legend by the Lady of Chalain), some of these houses have been recreated, and the photograph on page 9 shows what Pooley Bridge's first houses might have looked like. However, most of Ullswater was not suited for the type of home that had been so successfully employed by the Celts elsewhere, as the sides of the lake shoal quickly away into deep water. Thus the early settlers protected their homes by building them on the hillsides or tops of conical peaks.

Of all the early fortified settlements, that on the summit of Dumallard Hill (or Dunmallot/Dunmallet) is also the most significant. Most Ordnance Survey maps simply label the 775 feet (237 metres) summit with the words 'fort', but a close inspection of the conical shaped hill reveals its important strategic location at the entrance to Ullswater. Quite what the name Dunmallard means is not really clear. Although Dun means fortress, mallard can not refer to wildfowl, for the name 'fortress of the ducks' would hardly strike fear into anyone who had designs on attacking it. Dunmallard is therefore probably a corruption of Dunmalloght or Dunmallock.

In connection with other hilltops such as Great Mell Fell, Little Mell Fell, Heugh Scar Hill and The Riggs, Dunmallard may have formed a line of defensive locations that could have repelled any invader. In more ways than one, Pooley Bridge was the gateway to the Lakes. Just how large the settlement was around here we can only hazard a guess, but the ancient sites on the high ground of Askham Common and Barton Fell give some indication that habitation was probably extensive and of some considerable duration.

Dunmallard Hill is also called Dunmallet which may mean Fortress of the Hammer or Hill of Slaughter. The other possibilities are that it was named after a King of Cumberland called Mallok, a place of worship to the god Molech, or that it may be linked with the Gaelic word for curses Mallacht! It is said that the hill was once provided with a gruesome torture chamber, which would tie in nicely with the name meaning 'fort of the cursed'. The village nestling below this ancient settlement takes its name from the Norse language, and it means 'the hill with a pool'. It was formerly called Pool How or Pulhoue, names which stem from Pol or Pollr, and Haugr. It was later known as Powley or Poolah before becoming Pooley Bridge around 1800, although the bridge itself dates from the 16th-century. A feature of the village for many years (although no-one can be certain as to how long), was the important fish market. This may have been commenced in either the Celtic or Roman periods, but it was certainly active in Saxon times, and it is known that supplies were taken to local monasteries where the monks were prohibited from eating meat.

The trade carried on well into the Middle Ages, and there are records of fish merchants trading in the 18th century. Char was the main delicacy and some were processed in jelly and salt, but trout was also a staple part of the trade. Although it is now long gone, a telltale of the fish trade can still be found on a local weather vane if you look closely enough.

Most people come now for the tourism attractions, and in its own way Pooley Bridge has much to offer the visitor. Apart from the rows of grey stone houses in the village, there are some good hotels, including one of the finest in the world just a short distance down the lane to Howtown. The village also includes several shops for souvenirs and equipment for exploring the great outdoors, as well as good restaurants, pubs and the steamer service that provides links down the lake.

Pooley Bridge had its popular figures, and one (Colonel W. H. Parkin of Raven Crag) is still remembered by the Parkin Memorial Hall, which opened in February 1912. Another man of fame was a 17th century blacksmith, who was known as Strong Jack because of his great feats of prowess. His smithy was located in what is now a row of cottages opposite the local church, and traces of the grindstone stand and well are still evident. Yet another local man was the anti-slavery campaigner Thomas Clarkson who lived at a country house called Eusemire. His wife was a close friend of William and Dorothy Wordsworth and they often set out on walks together. One such walk was to the site of nearby Tristamount, which is believed to have been the home of King Arthur's ally, Sir Tristam.

This stunning view of Pooley Bridge in the 1950s, shows a pastoral scene beyond the village, rowing boats on the River Eamont, and Lady of The Lake *turning off the pier. The boat house in the woods, was the base for the 'secret' testing of miniature submarines during the war.* CG

Lovely, remote and beyond the electricity mains, the rugged buildings of Boredalehead Farm stand at the base of Hawk Crag with the stunning Place Fell beyond. ML

One of the most attractive parts of Ullswater, is the narrow strip of land on its south-eastern shore between Pooley Bridge and Howtown. Here a narrow belt of farmland, interspersed with fine country houses, gives way to the high escarpment leading up to Barton Fell and Bonscale. Camping sites and the local yacht club are found along the road, but undoubtedly the most famous 'tourist' facility is the renowned Sharrow Bay Hotel. Whilst it would be singularly unfair of this book to select any one hotel over the other splendid hotels on the lake, it is fair to say the Sharrow Bay has a worldwide reputation. Its superb location offers wonderful views, and by way of example we would point to the cover picture of this book which was taken from the lake's shore near the hotel.

Beyond Sharrow Bay the escarpment gets progressively steeper, as Barton Fell begins to climb up from White Knott towards Long Crag, Whinny Crag and Arthurs Pike. From this escarpment the Swarth Beck tumbles down in small cascades to enter the lake near Ravencragg. This lovely country house was the home of the Parkin family, but during World War II it became the home for the Lancashire & National Sea Training Home, which had been 'evacuated' from Wallasey in 1941.

Beyond Ravencragg the road leads to the small community of Howtown situated on the edge of Howtown Bay. Here will be found the third of the lake steamers' piers, which is situated in the shadow of the conical shaped Hallin Fell (1,271 feet - 388 metres). Like similar hills in the area, this attractive hill also has traces of early habitation and possible fortification.

The name Howtown incorporates both Celtic and Saxon terms, and it means 'the farmstead on the hill'. As modern Howtown is situated on ground that has built up around the estuary of the Fusedale Beck, we must assume that the name actually applies to a farm that was once situated on the higher ground above the lake. Some commentators believe that it may have been a fortified Viking farm settlement, the name Hallin being derived from Hallr, the Norse word for slope.

Unless you are taking part in one of the many outdoor activities arranged from the Howtown Outward Bound Centre, the village itself has little in the way of 'visitor facilities' with the exception of a very picturesque country hotel. It has traces of old industry though, and long before the tourists came the local watermill was used for a variety of purposes, though this was later converted to a bobbin mill in 1900.

ABOVE: *The Boredale and Bannerdale valleys are nearly as natural today as they have been for centuries, and fortunately this is helped by the sheer inaccessibility that places like Martindale Hause present to the big tour-coaches.* AE

BELOW: *The rugged Hallin Fell seen from Swarthfield.* AE

It is for the wider scenery that visitors flock in their thousands, with the majority sensibly arriving by boat. Having alighted at the pier, you immediately get the impression that you are in splendid isolation with a great adventure awaiting. Many will take the lake path back to Patterdale and Glenridding, passing Sandwick (one of the jewels of Ullswater) en-route. This community also has very ancient origins, but it is probably best known because its wholly Norse name means sandy bay/inlet.

The other big attractions for walkers alighting from the boat at Howtown are the wild wastes of Martindale Common and the twin valleys of Boredale and Bannerdale. To reach these you must take a series of hairpin bends up Martindale Hause, between Hallin Fell and Steel Knots. This is really worth the climb because it offers stunning views across the lake or into valleys (one such view is seen on the rear cover of the book). Fells such as Arthur's Pike or Swarth Fell are there for the more ambitious to climb, but the most gentle circular route is that skirting the foot of Hallin Fell, before reaching the lake at Sandwick.

Alternatively, if you climb to the summit of Martindale Hause, you will find one of the valleys' two churches nestling in a wooded glade just below the top of the pass. Beyond here you can descend an attractive narrow road (usually with Herdwick sheep for company) to reach the first hamlet around Hause Farm.

From here there is a choice of three roads to explore. Straight on takes you into the loveliest valley, Bannerdale, which includes the stream called Howe Grain, as well as Christy Bridge and a second church that dates back to the 16th-century. This church, St. Martin's, was built on the site of a church that was far older, possibly by as much as 700 or 800 years. The road serves Dale Head and, from here, it's into the fells. The Ramps Gill valley splits from Bannerdale at Dale Head Farm, but Bannerdale is the more-intriguing one, including an ancient settlement around a few metres off the track and quite near to Heck Beck.

However, if you, bear right at the first two junctions after coming over Martindale Hause you will reach Boredale instead. After around half a mile (800 metres) there is a sharp right-turn for the ancient and sleepy hamlet of Sandwick, where all the rivers and streams of Martindale empty into Ullswater, a factor that probably prompted the early inhabitants to extensively settle here.

The final Martindale option is to pass the Sandwick junction and head up Boredale to Boredale Head, from where the ancient trail to Patterdale begins. However, if you want to explore these valleys, please remember it is far better to leave the car behind and explore them on foot, using the Post Bus or lake steamer to get you to a suitable starting point.

INGLEWOOD

During the 'dark ages', much use was made of the old Roman road from Old Penrith (Voreda) to Keswick, initially by the post-Roman British who used it to protect the northern flanks of their homeland. Yet the dark wooded forests that fringed the road east of the Blencathra mountain range were also used by the Angles, Saxons and Vikings. However, it was with the coming of the Normans that the area assumed greater importance after William Rufus dispossessed Dolphin in 1092.

This event ended a 57 year Scottish military tenure of the area, which itself had come about after the Dunmail, King of Cumbria had been defeated in battle on the pass above Grasmere. To control the border the Normans formed a Palatine (buffer state) under Ranulph des Maschines. As part of this plan, came the establishment of three Baronies, a Royal Forest at Inglewood and a series of towers and castles along the course of what is now the A66 trunk road. The forest was very important in its own right and it was so extensive that its boundaries extended from the Eamont almost to Carlisle. In 1330 it was said to be 'uncultivated and infested with wild beasts', but by the days of Edward I it had been stocked with red and fallow deer in order to create a hunting park.

At the centre of the park stood a fortified house, Hutton-in-the-Forest, which is the legendary setting of the Green Knight's Castle in the Arthurian tale of Sir Gawain and The Green Knight. The house that stands there now has defined mediæval origins and the old Pele tower still survives. These buildings have, however, been altered by successive generations and the beautiful historic house that stands on the site today shows a wide range of architectural and decorative styles. These styles range from the 17th century onwards, and the house has been in the ownership of the Inglewood family since 1603.

Today the house and gardens are open to the public (unlike the castle at nearby Greystoke) and, with Dalemain, it makes an ideal venue if the weather is unkind. Yet along with its fine rooms and fascinating features (such as the Cupid Staircase), the house has much more to offer than shelter on a wet day. Perhaps you will want to explore the 18th century walled garden, with its stunning herbaceous borders. Alternatively you might wish to try the woodland walk, or attend one of the 'Meet The Gardener' sessions. Special events are also held from time to time, and what more natural setting could you wish for a performance of a Shakespearean play.

DALEMAIN

There has been an important house near the confluence of the Dacre Beck and River Eamont for well over 700 years. Meaning mansion in the valley, Dalemain was built around a 12th-century pele tower. It was probably raised by the de Morville's who were Lords of Westmorland, Knaresborough and Maulds Meaburn. One of this family, Sir Hugh de Morville, was an accomplice in the murder of Thomas a' Beckett at Canterbury Cathedral in 1170, and after this infamous event he sought refuge at Dalemain.

The de Morville's were followed by the Layton family, who are known to have been there in 1272. It was this family who extended the tower into a mediæval hall in 1400. From there it progressed to a manor house with two new wings being added in the days of Elizabeth I. However the Layton's ownership came to an end in the mid-17th century after the death of Sir William who fathered six daughters (but no son).

In 1679 the estate was bought by Sir Edward Hassell (chief steward to Lady Anne Clifford) for the sum of £2,710 (a 'snip' at around £150,000 in today's money). Yet the house required a great deal of work to befit the new owner (who was shortly to become the High Sheriff of Cumberland) and the current Georgian frontage of pink sandstone (quarried at Stainton) was completed by 1744. Despite this work the original buildings remained basically unchanged, and this intriguing house (with its fine museum and excellent gardens) is well worth visiting.

There are several grand Georgian public rooms including the wonderful Chinese Room, which still has its original, hand-painted Oriental wallpaper dating from 1750. Another intriguing feature of Dalemain, which has a total of 34 rooms, is its Tudor wing, which incorporates a glorious confusion of stairways and hidden rooms. Most fascinating is the Fretwork Room, which is bedecked with fine oak panelling and an original 16th century plaster ceiling. There is a wealth of quality furniture, family portraits, ceramics as well as the Museum of Cumberland Yeomanry in various rooms of the mansion. There is also the Mediæval Hall that is used today as a welcoming tea-room and restaurant.

The Hassell family continued to play a major role in the civil and political affairs of the area, with various members being High Sheriff's of both Cumberland and Westmorland. Involvement in the local militia was another function, and the Hassell's were prominent in the pursuit of the Jacobite rebels after the uprising of 1745. Another member of the family Lt. Colonel Edward Hassell (1795-1872) helped ensure local prosperity through his chairmanship of the Lancaster & Carlisle Railway. As the sixth Sir Edward had no male heirs, the house passed to his eldest daughter Sylvia Mary McCosh, who then worked tirelessly with her husband to restore the house and gardens. She passed away in 1991 but Dalemain and its lovely gardens remain a living testimony to this energetic lady.

Brougham Castle, sentinel at the gate to the Eamont Valley. EH

After the River Eamont leaves the lake it enters a broadening vale as it flows to join the River Eden near Langwathby. This is a historic and fascinating valley, but often ignored by the bulk of those visiting Ullswater. Its most popular site is undoubtedly the magnificent house at Dalemain, but the area contains a whole host of historic sites. For example Barton Church, which now looks like any other country church, but was once a major religious centre. The church was built around another Norman tower, and the nearby Church Hall Farm also has considerable antiquity. A little further along the village of Tirril is thought to be an old settlement, for this is where the Roman Road called High Street began its climb to the fells. The ancient mill at Sockbridge on the Eamont has had a varied history, but its tranquil setting now suits its role as a trout farm.

The valley has several fine old farms and yeoman's houses whilst Yanwath has two attractive country houses (both of which are private residences). The first of these is the Hall, built around the Pele tower erected by John de Sutton in 1322, the other bears the unusual name of the Grotto. One of its owners, Thomas Wilkinson (1751-1836), a friend of Wordsworth, gained distinction by walking to a Quaker meeting in London in 1791, doing the 300 miles (480 kms) or so in just eight days. Wilkinson was also a poet, and in addition to Wordsworth other renowned poets such as Thomas Clarkson, Thomas de Quincey, Sir Walter Scott and Charles Lloyd all stayed at the Grotto.

Where the B5320 joins the A6, is found the small but ancient community around Eamont Bridge. This has long been an important crossing place of the River Eamont, and evidences of its early history are clearly obvious. The name Eamont was derived from the old English 'ea' (or eau) for water and 'mont' for mountain or hill, and as one historian wrote in 1777 'people knew it flowed from a most mountainous country.' There was a ford across the river at the bottom of Kemplay Bank before the Romans came, but the first recorded bridge dates from the reign of Henry VI (1422-61). The present bridge across the river dates from the early 16th-century, and this fine structure is surrounded by a number of houses that date from the 18th-century.

Snuff manufacture was once an important industry round Ullswater with several local mills (including one near Dacre). The last was found in Eamont Bridge until it closed in 1937, when the old machinery was transferred to a factory in Kendal. The main employers today, apart from pubs and hotels, include a printing works based in the 1686-built Mansion House and Jubilee House, which is a convalescent home opened in 1995 by the British Firefighters' Benevolent Fund.

North of Eamont Bridge is the once-notorious Kemplay Bank, which used to have a dangerous hairpin bend on the A6 and many lorries ended up out-of-control when descending the hill. After a series of very bad accidents (including one during a thunderstorm in 1932), the road was straightened out in 1948. Yet, even during these remedial works a 35-ton lorry went out of control and crashed off the bridge into the river.

Eamont Bridge's most historic features are the King Arthur's Round Table, situated at the A6/B5320 junction, and Mayburgh Henge, just to the west. Both of these will be discussed in great detail in a future 'CUMBRIA HERITAGE' book, but we can not move on without giving a brief description of these two important sites.

Despite its name, Arthur's Round Table has no firm connection to the legend of King Arthur and his Knights, and it dates from the early-Bronze age of around 1,800 BC. The site, according to the notice board erected by English Heritage, shows it to be a prehistoric monument (probably) dating from between 2,000 and 1,000 BC. A wide ditch encloses a low circular platform, and beyond the ditch, there is an earthen bank. There is one entrance to the south-east which passes through both the bank and the ditch, but a similar entry-point to the north-west was obliterated during the construction of the road to Pooley Bridge.

Professor Collingwood extensively studied the site in 1937 and he suggested that the henge was either a temple or other religious gathering place, or possibly a burial ground for a prominent person. The discovery of a 'fire trench' on 17th June 1937, led to the belief that the site may also have served as a Bronze Age crematorium.

The highly-significant discovery of two pre-historic floors (one six to eight inches above the other), led Collingwood to believe that the Round Table was a product of two different eras and had been rebuilt years or even centuries after its first appearance. At the end of the excavation a triple circle layout of wooden posts had been traced, and the 'fire-trench' was confirmed as a crematorial feature, built into the 'second floor level' after it yielded charcoal deposits and calcinated pieces of bone which were most likely included during a rebuilding of the henge.

The theory was that the bones belonged to one of the Kings of Rheged, or possibly a King of all England, but certainly an important ancient chieftain. In any case it was something different from the usual Neolithic graves, where entire families or clan members tended to be buried in communal graves. A second 'dig' in 1939 found evidence of four different periods of occupation, not just two! However, it was also recognised that the construction of the Crown Hotel, on the opposite side of the road in 1770, had severely harmed the ancient henge.

ABOVE: *English Heritage describes Mayburgh Henge as a massive prehistoric monument measuring 120 metres across, including the banking. It is connected with the ancient Druids sometime between 1,500 and 2,000 BC, and it would have existed (like Arthurs Round Table) near the junction of several important trade routes, and close to the ford over the Eamont. There is not a lot of the site left today, except the single standing stone and the entrance through the banking on the east. Even so, you can marvel at the feat of ancient engineering, and imagine just how difficult it was to build it up from the huge stones that they undoubtedly hauled from the River Eamont.*

By the end of the excavations it was being thought that stone pillars might have been used to hold a thatched roof, only to be later 'quarried' for use in local walls or buildings. The stones, it was suggested, would have replaced earlier wooden pillars in one of the rebuilding operations.

But where does its name come from? The fact that a Roman Gallienus coin was discovered on the site, gave rise to the suggestion that the henge had remained in use for many years, and that it may well have had some connection with the post-Roman era when Arthur is thought to have lived in the area.

Nearby is the ancient site of Mayburgh Henge, which probably dates from around 2,000 BC. This consists of a high outer mound marked out with trees and is reckoned to have been a late-Neolithic religious gathering place, possibly a temple or court of combat. It used to contain two concentric stone circles of which only one stone, around 16 feet (5m) tall, remains. According to *The History and Antiquities of the Counties of Cumberland & Westmorland*, (1777), 'the Henge used to be called Mayborough Castle and was almost in the shape of a horse-shoe with a central area of 88 yards in diameter.' Its main entrance is on the north-east side, and had consisted of a single 'rampier' of stones which by 1777 had already been reduced to rubble and overgrown with trees.

Many of the large stones were 'dressed' on the site and hauled away for vital repairs to Penrith Castle during the reign of King Henry VI (1422-1461). However, at least one large stone was left in place, slightly west of the centre of the monument where it stands today (actually one report states that there were still at least eight standing-stones on the site in the 18th century).

Just south of Eamont Bridge, is Brougham Hall Farm the site of the annual Penrith Agricultural Show which has taken place here every July since 1966, although it was held in various places after the local Agricultural Society was launched in 1834. On a high bluff above this farm stands Brougham Hall, which was formerly the home of Henry Brougham who has been described as 'one of the best five Lord Chancellors England ever had.' After being allowed to go into dereliction the Hall has since been restored and now serves as a crafts centre, museum and Alice's Wonderland Doll Museum.

A little further we come to Brougham Castle, which commands a vantage point over the confluence of the Eamont and Lowther rivers. The castle, now in the care of English Heritage, was commenced around 800 years ago by Robert de Veteripont to fend off invaders from Scotland, but its most famous resident was Lady Anne Clifford. Daughter of Henry (described by Shakespeare as 'The Bloody Clifford'), Anne became Countess of Pembroke and she is still remembered with affection by the people of Westmorland because she undertook considerable work to restore the buildings and the estates she inherited from her father.

Her re-building of the castles at Appleby and Brougham were amongst her major achievements and she lived at Brougham for 25 years, from 1651 to her death in March 1676. In 1654 she erected the octagonal Countess Pillar in memory of her final parting with her mother on 2nd April 1616. Each anniversary of this event sees a small unusual ceremony taking place at 12 noon, when money known as the 'Brougham Dole' is handed out to the poor of the parish. In the modern cutting that takes the A66T below the pillar, a significant Roman burial ground was discovered during the road construction works in 1966.

Up to the east of the castle is Whinfell Forest, which has both Celtic and Viking connections but was made famous in local legend due to the chase of a stag from the woods to the head of Ullswater and back in the days of Richard Duke of Gloucester. Today the forest is better known as the site of the Oasis Forest holiday village complex. Continuing along the Eamont, and reached by a delightful walk from the A66T, is the small church of St. Ninians or Ninekirks. Built opposite the place where this early Christian missionary had his frugal 'cell' in a cave above the river, and preached to the locals.

The church (built by Lady Anne in 1660) is still used for special services, and above the alter it contains a copy of the tetragramaton (YHWH), the Hebrew word for God's name, which is Yahweh or Jehovah. It is one of the few religious buildings in the land where the sacred inscription was retained, as many removed it in the late-middle ages in the erroneous belief that its use was blasphemous.

The last Eamont landmark is the historic Hornby Hall (now a guest house) and part of the Winderwath Estate which in turn has links with the Norse settlers of 1,000 years ago. On certain summer days, the gardens of Winderwath house are open to the public. Between Hornby Hall and Winderwath the Eamont joins the Eden at Waters Meet near Langwathby. In really wet weather this confluence floods and creates a really spectacular sight as the rivers form a huge, swirling lake, which can be viewed from the Langwathby road.

Going in the other direction (south on the A6 from Eamont Bridge) takes you to Clifton which has, as its main claim to fame, the site of the last Anglo-Scottish battle ever fought on English soil. The battle took place on the night of 18th December 1745, when the Duke of Cumberland's force caught up with the Jacobites being led by the legendary Bonnie Prince Charlie.

Sick of the tyranny over Scotland, the Jacobites had sought to take control of Britain, depose King George I from power and restore the Stuart's to the throne. The 'risings' of 1709 and 1715 fizzled out due to a lack of support in Scotland but, by 1745, and with King George II now on the English throne, the young Bonnie Prince Charlie whipped up enough support for a march on London with armed soldiers.

Having crossed the border into England the Scots seized

ABOVE: *The little known visitor attraction of Clifton Hall, maintained by English Heritage, which is just off the A6 at Clifton. The Manor of Clifton dates from around 1170, when the lands were granted to Gilbert d'Engaine. The tower pictured here dates from c1500.* LE

Carlisle without much ado before going south. After resting at Penrith on the night of 22nd November, the army eventually reached Derby on 4th December, but were then compelled to head back north after hearing that the Duke of Cumberland's Redcoats were being mustered against them. They then retreated in separate groups, and the last group got to Clifton late on the 18th. Tired of running, and still 35 miles south of the border, they decided to set an ambush. As the Redcoats reached the village, the rebels pounced on them in a Highland Charge. The ensuing fight led to the deaths of around 15 troops from either side. A Lieutenant Colonel Honywood, of Howgill Castle, fighting for the English side, was set upon so violently that his helmet was pierced in nine separate places. Not surprisingly, it came off to reveal several wounds to his head, but he survived and was later promoted to Lt.General.

The battle involved only a few hundred retreating Scots and thousands of English, but the Jacobites took credit in a moral victory and retreated to Carlisle. Today two historic sites that are open to the public are to be found nearby, namely Clifton Hall (a fortified Pele Tower) and the fascinating Wetheriggs Country Pottery at Clifton Dykes.

There is so much to say about Lowther and Askham in the story of Ullswater, but sadly so little room to say it! Connected strongly with the Lowther family, the best known examples (as far as visitors are concerned) are Lowther Park (a leisure park offering three types of family attraction), Lowther Caravan Park, the Bird of Prey Centre and the Lowther Horse trials held annually each August. Yet the most impressive sight are the ruins of the once grandeous Lowther Castle which was designed by Robert Smirke, the designer of the British Museum. Although only the frontage of the Castle is still standing it was once one of the north's greatest buildings. At its height the castle staff employed large numbers of domestics, including 50 to 60 gardeners and about the same amount of gamekeepers. Built between 1806 and 1811, it often had Royal visitors, including the German Kaiser Wilhelm in 1895.

The Emperor's host was the best-known Earl of Lonsdale, Hugh Cecil Lowther (the 5th Earl - 1857-1944), who was affectionately known as the 'Yellow Earl' because of his love of the colour. Quite apart from being noted for his connections with boxing (through his award of the Lonsdale Belt) his many other achievements included being the close friend of Kings and Emperors. He was also a great sportsman and had even taken part in an Arctic expedition between 1888 and 1889, in which he trekked thousands of miles by foot or on dogsled, returning via San Francisco in April 1889. He also formed the Lonsdale Battalion, but it suffered huge losses during the Great War (1914-1918). He married Lady Grace Cicelie Gordon in 1878 and the couple's Golden Wedding party in 1928 was attended by none other than King George V and Queen Mary. Despite his privileged status, he was also known to be a good friend to commoners as well as kings.

Yet despite this, the Lowthers had to 'close' the Castle on 1st January 1936 due to its high running costs. After the outbreak of war the grounds were requisitioned by the army and used for training, following which a huge sale of the contents took place in 1947; these even attracted the film magnate Alexander Korda, who bought some of the castle's carriages for use in his films. Sadly the castle was stripped of its lavish interior, roof and floors in 1957 after attempts to sell it to pay off the Yellow Earl's death duties (said to total £2,000,000) failed.

Between the castle and the beautiful village of Askham, stands Askham Hall (the present Lowther residence). This private home, mostly hidden amidst the trees, has a Pele tower that dates from the 14th century. The main part is an Elizabethan mansion built in 1574 by Thomas Sandford.

THE LIFE-SAVERS OF PATTERDALE

Few visitors to the Ullswater area ever anticipate that they would need the services of the local rescue team, or could end up like this picture shows, secured to a Bell Stretcher on a crag high above the lake. Unfortunately, each year the Lakeland fells contrive to catch out the unwary, local and visitor alike. Despite their magnificent beauty and great attraction, these are far from hospitable environments. For centuries people have had to face situations with potentially tragic consequences. Yet when human souls are in peril, there is something in the heart of men that will encourage them to put life and limb at risk in order to help their fellow. The Patterdale Mountain Rescue Team continue the fine tradition, and they practice regularly for every possible contingency such as seen here. PMRT

ABOVE: *The work of the team necessitates the ability to reach victims as quickly as possible, and whilst much high-level work can only be done on foot, the team also need to get their equipment and members as close to the scene as possible. As shown here, their well-equipped Land Rover ambulances can easily cover steep ground when needed.* PMRT

Bbelow: *In recent years much more use has been made of 'rescue dogs' along with the Search & Rescue Dog Association (SARDA). This picture of another exercise demonstrates the effectiveness of the animals at discovering 'victims'.* PMRT

When these hills began to attract mountaineers and fell-walkers, anyone who came to grief would be rescued by a mix of farmers, huntsmen and the local police; the people who knew the area best.

The fact that such people were (and still are) best-suited for these tasks is shown by the story of a woman who failed to arrive at her destination after setting out from Grasmere to Patterdale in August 1922. When the 'alarm' was raised, the village 'bobby' organised a search party that was comprised of the noted Patterdale huntsman Joe Bowman and 11 local men. Regretfully, their search ended in tragedy, when they found that the woman had died of exposure. This event prompted the *Cumberland & Westmorland Herald* to call for the formation of a Mountain Rescue Brigade. Unfortunately it was left to the locals for forty more years, before the idea became a reality. The explosion of tourism in the 1950s, with its attendant 'mountain accidents' led to repeated suggestions for a rescue team.

The impetus finally came from the local GP, Dr. James Davis Ogilvie, who had moved to Patterdale from Kent just as the Lake District was 'thawing out' after a bad winter. Even so, then as now, people were setting out for the hills unprepared for the savage conditions that could be encountered. The series of incidents that took place around this time soon led the doctor to declare that he had seen enough of the needless injuries that he was having to treat. These incidents, and the frequency with which other locals were being 'enlisted' to help in cases of emergency, convinced him there was a real case for founding a Mountain Rescue Team in the Ullswater area.

With his proposals gathering momentum, 20 people attended a meeting at the Glenridding Public Hall on 2nd October 1964. Under the doctor's enthusiastic chairmanship, the Patterdale Mountain Rescue Team was formed. That original Team comprised a total of 27 members, including Dr. Ogilvie and two members of his family, while his wife was on the Committee. The Team's first year saw 14 call-outs, with two fatal incidents. The first winter was a stern test of the new organisation, but in August 1966 they achieved their first major goal when they opened their new HQ at Deer Howe, a former barn given to them rent-free by the Patterdale Hotel.

Remaining as Team Leader for eight years, Dr. Ogilvie retired from the post in 1973, the same year that the Team recruited their first search-and-rescue dog Sultan. The Team had many call-outs in his time, including one involving a party of schoolboys who were climbing with their headmaster in the hills around Blea Tarn, above Haweswater, on 9th October 1972. After a dislodged boulder crashed down on them one boy was killed outright and three others were badly injured, as they were dragged down the scree slopes by the debris. The team still describe this incident as one of the most difficult they have ever attended, and it also involved the teams from Penrith and the Ullswater Outward Bound Mountain School. The following day Dr. Ogilvie trekked back to the scene and recovered several pieces of bone from one victim's leg following a special request from the orthopaedic surgeon at the Cumberland Infirmary in Carlisle.

The vital pieces were found and, once the worst of the boy's injuries had healed, these bits of bone were remarkably grafted back into place in January 1973.

It is not just high-level incidents that the team has had to face, and even low-lying locations like Aira Force have posed their problems. At this popular beauty spot a climber had fallen and landed precariously on a crag part way down a steep slope. He had suffered serious back injuries, and was in danger of slipping further still. The awkward position in which the victim had fallen and a plague of mosquitoes hampered the rescue, but the most difficult problem was how to fit the spinal supports. The team managed to extricate the victim without aggravating his injuries however, and before too long he was on the way to the Spinal Injuries Unit. Two years later the fallen climber had recovered sufficiently enough to be able to go fell walking again, even if he did need a walking stick.

One of the biggest dangers facing those who take up outdoor pursuits is hypothermia, and in this field Dr. Ogilvie became a pioneer. He studied exposure and how it affected the human body, and then described for others how to recognise the symptoms of hypothermia and how to limit its effects. He also drew to the attention of mountaineers the equally serious Wind-Chill Factor, which comes from exposure to winds that are a lot colder than the predicted or 'recorded' temperature. Ogilvie also helped change age-old attitudes that it was 'the done thing' to toughen youngsters by exposing them to extreme conditions.

In 1969 the 'Doc' himself was badly injured while out rock-climbing on Harter Fell with a colleague when loose rock gave way on him and he fell 60 feet, injuring his head and back. Yet this did not limit his mountaineering activities, and he maintained his links with the Patterdale Mountain Rescue Association, eventually becoming its President. In 1983, some 20 years after arriving on the scene, Dr. Ogilvie reluctantly decided it was time to leave his beloved Lakes and returned to Kent. With reflection it is easy to see how much he accomplished in that time, but who would have thought it at the time. On 18th January 1996 this remarkably dedicated man passed away at his home in the South of England, but in accord with his wishes he returned to Cumbria that May when his ashes were scattered on Helvellyn.

Ironically the following month, the team he formed attended their 1,000th call out when a 15-year-old schoolgirl from Preston, Lancashire, lost her footing whilst walking. On the afternoon of Saturday, 29th June 1996 the girl fell heavily, sustaining facial and back injuries. She lay with friends until the team arrived at the scene above Howtown. As ever, they carefully treated the external wounds and then gently placed her on a special mattress designed for back-injury patients, before transferring her to hospital by helicopter.

There have been other memorable events over the years, and the highlights that follow are but a brief testimony to the work of the team. In July 1980 a nest full of buzzard chicks in the Helvellyn area triggered a call-out when calling for their parents (and food) by chirping in a way that sounded remarkably like the international distress signal. A party of Scouts heading down the mountain raised the 'alarm' after hearing a noise that sounded like six whistle blasts, repeated at intervals. The team turned out, as they always will and even false alarms are given very careful attention; for example in 1998 reports of flares and flashing lights prompted 'turnouts' on different occasions.

The weekend of 13-15th January 1984 was dubbed by some as a 'black weekend on a very-white Helvellyn', and it stretched the Patterdale Mountain Rescue Team pretty much to its limits. Four years later on 6-7th February 1988, they were called out on no less than 14 incidents, some of which were fatal ones.

In June 1992 a mountain-biker, who had injured his leg in a fall at Silver Point, became part of a 'double rescue'. As he was being taken by the Team's Rescue Boat to meet an ambulance at Glenridding, the crew were called to the aid of a female yachtsman, who had been pitched into the water after her dinghy capsized. On Sunday 16th January 1994, the team had seven call-outs in one day. These included a fatal heart attack at Hobcarton Crag, a fractured leg on Helvellyn, a spinal injury at Red Tarn, and a climber who had failed to make it to the top of a 'snow-climb' in the Grisedale Valley area. When his companion arrived at the team's base he was unable to tell them which mountain they were climbing, but after a lot of questions the team decided it was St. Sunday Crag, and duly found the missing man in the valley below.

In February 1995 the team attended a boy of 14 who had been injured in a fall in the snow on Catstye Cam, he had only bruised his head, but it could have been far, far worse. Quite beyond belief, the leaders of this boy's group had absolutely no experience of winter conditions on the fells and had irresponsibly left the youngsters unattended as they explored the Helvellyn range.

It is not only modern problems that the team are called to deal with, as was seen in July 1995 when a 'live' explosive device (left over from wartime army training) was discovered by a walker at High Street. This person alerted the team who were called out to search for the device, once they had located it, they guarded it (at a safe distance) until it could be dealt with safely by an Army Bomb Disposal Team.

The Team often attends less serious incidents too, including giving first aid to someone who had caught their hand in a minibus door, and rescuing a drunk from the beck in Glenridding!

Today the Teams' area covers some 140sq kilometres of the

Its members come from all walks of life giving their services entirely voluntarily, a tradition they are proud to maintain. The Team is available and 'on call' for 24 hours a day, 365 days a year. Members hold the Mountain First Aid Certificate, Off-Road Driving qualifications, Royal Yacht Association Power Boat Certificates and are experienced in Search Management Techniques. Today, the Patterdale Team members have to go through a 'rolling programme' of stringent tests, hospital-based training and certificate courses to ensure they are fit and qualified for the task. There are regular practice 'drills' for the Team and in 1997 some 61 call outs were logged.

When an emergency arises, call-outs begin with a '999' call to the police who in turn summon the Mountain Rescue team(s). Team members are summoned on radio-pagers, and on call out they will drop everything and race to offer their help. The team includes doctors and nurses, and they carry with them the same kind of emergency equipment that will be found in a Paramedic ambulance.

When they arrive at the accident site, either on foot or with their Land Rover Ambulance, they can rely on equipment such as a defibrillator - or 'Heart-start' machine. Modern technology now also enables them to transmit data on the patient's condition direct to the hospital, via a portable fax machine and phone, saving vital minutes by letting the medical team know in advance of injury and illness. Modern equipment does not come cheap, and the volunteers must find around £750 for each computer-programmed radiophone.

The biggest project has been the building of a new base, in order to provide the much-needed medical facilities they are now giving to a greater number of countryside users. To meet the demands of the next millennium, the new centre is designed to provide the highest standard of on-site care and will include a dedicated quiet area for friends or family of the casualty, a control room with the latest communications technology, and security for vehicles and equipment. It will also have an indoor training area and facilities to educate both school groups and the general public in mountain safety.

The National Lottery Sports Fund has granted £187,000 towards the £345,000 centre but every penny counts. If you want to help donations can be made in the collection boxes found locally, even the smallest coins will help maintain the work of this professional and dedicated team. Mind you, they much prefer the donations that can be folded, as this volunteer service can not be provided on a shoestring. Even when the centre is completed, donations will be vital to keep up the team's work (currently running around £20,000 per annum). It is the same with the neighbouring teams, such as those at Penrith and Keswick, all of whom regularly risk their own lives to help perfect strangers. They really need your help, but you can help them most of all by keeping out of trouble and avoid taking needless risks!

highest land in England, including Helvellyn, High street, Fairfield, St Sunday Crag and the wild beauty of Dovedale and Deepdale. The team's 'patch' also contains some of the great classic climbs of the area, and to the east of Ullswater the lonely countryside round Martindale and Riggindale complete an area of dramatic landscape. Each year the Team deals with an average of 60 call-outs, the majority of which involve hill walkers or climbers, although paragliders, mountain bikers and runners all figure in the statistics. They also respond to the needs of the local community when snow or floods hamper the conventional rescue services. It also assists local farmers in animal rescues, and one of its most spectacular call-outs was to 24 'crag-fast' foxhounds at St. Sunday Crag. Although the team had to wait until daylight before effecting the rescue, a system of ropes and a human chain eventually enabled them to pass the dogs down to safety one by one.

Lead Mining Around Ullswater

Greenside Mine. SM

Even though it may not appear so at first inspection, the upper part of the Ullswater valley has a long industrial past as we mentioned previously. For centuries the Glenridding Valley was associated with the lead mining industry, as a visit to the local information centre will reveal. Here (not far from the site of the largest of the valley's mines, Greenside), a section of the centre is dedicated to the days when the area was extensively worked for its mineral wealth. The permanent display at the centre shows how the industry impacted on the area and spurred the growth of Glenridding. Meanwhile two books on lead mining, *The Greenside Mines* and *Grey Gold*, are on sale locally for those who wish to know more.

As mentioned on page 14, the rocks that make up the local land formations contain many faults, and in these faults were formed the mineral deposits that gave birth to the lead mining industry. The science of mineralisation is very complex indeed, but the formation of minerals like galena (ore-bearing lead), copper, zinc and pyrite, came about through a process called skarning. Essentially mineral-laden ground water penetrated the faults in the bedrock, in turn this circulated down to great depths picking up more minerals and so on. The water then reached a depth where it became superheated and travelled towards the surface as steam or flows of heavily mineralised brine in which were included minute elements of heavy metals.

In turn these copious flows interacted and reacted with the surrounding rocks in which crystallisation had taken place as the ground water had percolated downwards. As this scalding hot water and steam cooled down, the heavy metal elements were deposited in large quantities within the crystalline materials such as quartz, calcite and barytes. Because these deposits took place in the faults and fractures that already existed in the rocks, the minerals would run in any direction. The miners called them strings, ribbons, pipes and flats, but they rarely went in a horizontal seam like coal.

Along with the lead and semi-precious metals a variety of gangue (waste) materials were formed. This gangue often contained beautiful crystal, which the miners would take for ornamental purposes. Surrounding the lead, other minerals such as zinc and barytes were found, but in the early days these had little value so they were just dumped in the waste heaps as the miners toiled to extract the copper and lead.

From the lead a small quantity of silver could be extracted, but this was often an uneconomic practice at many mines. Greenside was an exception, and the high silver content was such as to finance speculative explorations. The work on new levels (tunnels), shafts and sumps through the hard bedrock took years, and the veins of lead were not easily reached. Sometimes they were never found at all, and after thousands of hours had been expended a trial would be simply abandoned.

However, it was not uncommon for these trials to be picked

up again in later years, and sometimes these were pursued through to a successful conclusion. More often than not however, the trials were unsuccessful. Fortunately, like the oil exploration industry of today, it was the strikes in the mother load that paid for all the other speculative work.

Exactly when mining commenced in the Ullswater area can not be determined, and it may well be that man has dug out the metal where the veins were exposed at the surface since the Bronze-age. There is also great argument about how far north the Romans mined lead in Great Britain, although it is now generally accepted that they mined in the Peak District of Derbyshire, the Yorkshire Dales and the nearby North Pennines. There is debate about whether the Romans mined in the Lakes counties, but we must bear in mind that their mining operations were widespread in metal-producing parts of their empire. Looking at the route of the Roman roads in Cumbria, one can draw the striking conclusion that many of them went through (or very close to) the mining sites that later developed. A little to the east of Ullswater, Roman pigs of lead have been found alongside the A66 near Brough and Stainmore, though we can not prove from where they actually originated.

Following the Roman withdrawal, the lead industry was continued by German labourers who the Romans had introduced to British mines, but this seems to have declined before the end of the Saxon era. There was a considerable extraction of lead in the Norman era, but again we have no documentary evidence to support how much mining took place in the Lakes. There was considerable work undertaken on Alston Moor not many miles to the east, and we have definite evidence that lead mining was taking place on the Caldbeck Fells behind Blencathra in the 1300s

The next big mining boom in the lead industry again came with German miners who began taking up leases in Britain during the Elizabethan period, and records of these workings are quite well documented. Although local legend contends that the mines around Ullswater were worked at this time, there is nothing in the record to confirm this as being so. Unfortunately, in almost every mining district, traces of early mining, be they Bronze Age, Roman, Norman or Elizabethan, were subsequently obliterated by the extensive mining that took place in the 18th and 19th centuries.

Greenside Mine was the ultimate development of the small-scale mining that had been carried on by local people around Patterdale, Deepdale and Hartsop, and the mine reached a final depth of 237 fathoms below the Lucy Level. As a fathom is six feet, this was 1,422 feet (434 metres), all cut through hard rock. In total the mine reached a depth of 2,750 feet (838.75 metres). This work went on from around the 1690s to the 1960s, and for many years the people of the upper end of the valley were totally reliant on the Greenside mines.

Long before tourism became the staple industry, the high percentage of silver that was being extracted from local mines (around 15 to 30 ounces from each ton of ore) made this one of the most important mining villages in Britain. Situated in the foothills of Helvellyn, the mines made fortunes for some but led others into bankruptcy. One of the earliest recorded leases was for a mine at Hartsop, where Sir Nathaniel Johnson and Robert Jopling signed a 21-year lease in April 1696. Allied to the mining industry was the business of separating the mineral from the bedrock, and then smelting the lead.

In 1822 the Greenside Mining Company was formed, and by 1826 production at the mine had gone into full swing following viability trials. A major development was the Lucy Tongue Level that was proposed in 1853, and estimated to need around 20 years for completion. The full length of the new level was to be nearly a mile long to the Smith Shaft which was, as may be imagined, a very costly operation. Simultaneous with the construction of the 7 foot high level, the company undertook the rebuilding of the smelt mill.

Work progressed swiftly, despite the difficult conditions, and by the end of 1856 the Lucy Level had penetrated the hillside by a total of 130 fathoms. In the same period, other workings and newly discovered seams in the mine had rewarded the operators with almost 24,000 tons of lead. Work continued steadily up to the end of 1867, and by the end of the year rails were being laid in order to carry out the ore. In the hills above Greenside a six acre tarn at Kepple Cove was extended in capacity to provide water for the mine and smelter. In 1928 it was extended again with a dam 50 feet high (15 metres) by 150 feet long (46 metres) after the old dam had burst in 1927.

As the 19th-century drew to a close, the company invested in hydroelectricity generating. Using nature's power, water was fed through a system of turbines in order to generate power for the work. These were the first innovations of their kind in any metalliferous mine in the country, and the lighting must surely have been a lot better too. Another feature of electrification came in 1893, when an electric locomotive took over the work of seven horses on the subterranean rails.

Where shafts sank vertically in the mine, these were not worked down from the surface, and the winding gear was placed underground within the levels. In Lucy Level the first shaft was situated around a mile in from the entrance, and these then penetrated the seams of lead. Below the Lucy Level other levels, sumps and shafts would be sunk to intercept the veins. Extracting the minerals was hard work, and a variety of methods were used over the years, ranging from hand drills and gunpowder to modern compressed-air drills.

On the surface the work of dressing the ore, crushing the lead and smelting took place over a wide area. A tangible reminder of these operations can still be seen in the course of the smelt mill flue that ran for 1.5 miles up the mountainside.

The value of the industry can be shown by the figures for

1872, when the total of pig-lead production was 1,156 tons. This was worth £26,588 back then, but in modern prices it would be around one and a quarter million pounds, whilst silver production amounted to £4,335 (£206,012 at today's prices). In 1911 the year's pig lead amounted to 3,091 tons and was worth £39,499 (£2,266,729). According to a booklet entitled *British Lead Mines*, the overall amounts for Greenside up to 1876 were staggering. This showed that since its inception the firm had produced a total of 60,000 tons of lead yielding 40,000 tons of smelted lead worth £800,000 at 1876 prices (about £41,592,800) and 600,000 ounces of silver worth £150,000 (£7,798,650). With such riches to be had, employment was almost continuous (despite the rise and fall in lead prices). Consequently, numerous miners migrated to Ullswater from other mining districts in search of employment and this may be confirmed by an entry from as early as 1754, when the death of Derbyshire miner George Smedley is entered in the parish record.

Business was lucrative during periods of war, as lead was in great demand for munitions. Getting lead out of the area was always a problem, and it is probable that the early speculators made use of boats on Ullswater as well as strings of packhorses known as 'Galloway Trains'. The opening of the Troutbeck station on the Cockermouth, Keswick & Penrith Railway enabled the company to move its produce more easily and special sidings were allocated for lead traffic. The 20th century was started with confidence, the mine was still rich and it had a number of advantages over its neighbours on the Alston Moor.

Yet it also had its problems as for example, Kepple Cove Dam that claimed a victim on the night of 1st December 1902, when a miner slipped into the tarn and drowned. It happened during a raging storm when the man had gone to inspect the sluice, but after this Kepple Cove attracted a great deal of superstition and miners tended to keep clear of the place on dark winter nights. This was not without good reason for even this low part of the mountain is dangerous in a storm, but in the dead of winter its hazardous nature was well proven.

In 1903 the company stopped the extraction of silver, as by this time it had become no longer profitable. The period during World War I was not as productive as one would think because, despite the spiralling demand for lead, many of the miners were called up for military service. As a consequence output fell dramatically and lead had to be purchased from a competitor in order for the company to maintain the production quota set by the Ministry of War Supply. By 1918 the smelt mill's days were numbered, and its closure that year foreshadowed the troubles facing the company. In 1919 the mine's fortunes were in a deplorable state, and papers were filed for liquidation. Work carried on however, and in 1923 a new company was formed with sufficient cash to keep the business going. Even so no one had reckoned with the disaster of Bonfire Night (5th November) 1927. During the early hours of that Saturday night severe gales and torrential rain lashed the fells around Ullswater and water levels in Kepple Cove Reservoir began to rise. It was a wild violent night, but following the earlier tragedy of 1902, it seems that the task of checking the sluices at night was not always carried out.

ABOVE: *An underground view of work in the Greenside Mine c1900. These mines provided so much of the wealth for the village, and due to their very high productivity they were able to survive much longer than lead mines in other areas.* SM

BELOW: *The entrance to the Lucy Level at Greenside seen in the 1950s, showing the mine's railway wagons (tubs) waiting to go underground.* GRC

A five and a half day week was worked up to the outbreak of hostilities, but thereafter the mine was worked flat out. Labour was quite a problem, and to address this situation a number of prisoners of war were conscripted into working at Greenside. In 1943 a number of Canadian Army Engineers were brought to work at Greenside. Around the same time the electric locomotive of 1937 was converted to battery power as problems were being encountered from the Mines Inspectorate, who raised safety concerns about the locomotive's overhead electric supply.

Even though this had never been a problem in the working of the mine, an electrical incident was to cause a disaster when the mine returned to full working after the war. It occurred on 7th July 1952 when an electrical fire commenced at the 200 fathom level, and this in turn filled the galleries and shafts with deadly carbon monoxide. Unaware of the dangers a shift of 36 men entered the workings and four of these were to become victims of the fumes, with several more being overcome.

By 1954 the mine was still producing around 25,000 tons of raw ore, of which 2,000 tones of concentrate were being sent by rail to Newcastle where it was processed; but by 1959 the geological reports indicated a bleak future for Greenside. Around this time an agreement was reached with the Atomic Weapons Research Establishment at Aldermaston, who were seeking to simulate an atomic explosion at a depth of around 1,000 feet (320 metres). The tests were duly carried out way below Sheffield Pike, and with appropriate compensation paid to the firm work commenced on rebuilding the mine in 1960. As this work was being carried out, two miners went to explore the old workings to look for crystals, but on entering one of the side drives they were overcome by a pocket of gas. It was just one of the final and tragic acts at Greenside, and in April 1961 the very last tub of ore was extracted. The mine finally closed on 31st January 1962 and thereafter the site was levelled of buildings and the entrances sealed.

An enormous amount of waste and spoil still litter the hillsides above the mine, and the LDNPA continually work on the site to prevent erosion and landslide. Today most of the lower mine workings are flooded with clear blue water, and the other workings are silent but for the dripping of water. Yet, with official sanction, exploration of the workings has been allowed, and in turn this has aided the production of two aforementioned books that will help modern visitors understand this now defunct industry.

Yet on this occasion a watchman might just have been alerted to the fact that the winds were rapidly stirring up the waters in the 8-acre reservoir. As these waves battered the dam it was quickly overwhelmed, and this in turn caused a breach in the banking at a weak point. As a result, millions of gallons of water cascaded three miles down the valley towards Glenridding, and gathering speed it tore up rocks, bushes and trees as it went. Below people slept soundly in their beds, until the cascade of water and debris smashed into the unwitting village in total darkness. Even animals grazing in the fields were caught completely unawares, especially those at Eagle Farm. Here the water caused major damage and deaths of livestock. At 7am the following morning, the keeper of the Dam (who lived well away from the path the water took) finally went to check all was well at the start of his shift. Clearly unaware of the mayhem, he was stunned to find the reservoir was almost totally empty. The problems of the flood damage forced the company into paying out huge sums in compensation, and this was followed by the Wall Street Crash in October 1929. By 1934 the price of lead was at an all-time low, standing at around half the price it had been fetching just prior to the war. Only bankruptcy could follow.

However in 1936 the Basinghall Mining Company took over Greenside. Their engineer's report indicated good prospects, especially as the world rushed towards rearmament and problems grew with National-socialist Germany. Early in 1937 the mine was fitted out with new equipment and supplies, including a new electric locomotive. By summer the work was under way and it was anticipated that production would be in excess of 250 tons per day.

PROTECTING THE LAKES

The attractive Glencoyne Valley, with its ancient farmstead, which was saved for the 'nation' by the National Trust. AE

There have long been concerns about the very special environment of the Lake District, and for centuries enlightened men and women have been highlighting the area's unique character, and pointing out that it was worthy of control and protection. This became especially so as the industrial revolution, with its dark satanic mills and sprawling railway lines, were burgeoning all over Britain. From the early days people like Wordsworth, Ruskin and others, began moves to protect their beloved Lake District, particularly from the all-invading railway. Ironically, many of the railway plans that these men were so successful in defeating would, today, form the solution to Lakeland's traffic problems. Notwithstanding that incontrovertible fact, those early protectors recognised that industrial encroachment of the Lakes could not be permitted.

The focal point of this campaign might be acknowledged as one Canon Rawnsley, a cleric who might be correctly viewed as the 'Father of the National Trust'. Following his early efforts, bodies like the National Trust, Friends of The Lake District, The Lake District National Park Authority and others, have since got together with landowners and recreation users.

As we have already mentioned it took a bold move in 1929

to present the message that the Lake District was a very special place and needed proper protection, for there were so many vested interests to consider. At an early stage there was a call for 'National Park' status, but a period of severe economic pressure in the 1920s and 1930s followed by World War II meant that this status was not achieved until the 1949 National Parks & Access to Countryside Act was passed by the first post-war Labour government.

On the creation of the National Park a management body (now called the LDNPA) was set up, and their fine work continues down to the present. With consultation, debate and sometimes argument, the authority have done much to achieve the best means of preserving the area's natural character.

Obviously this has not been an easy task, as so many demands are placed upon this special environment, some of the issues have been resolved by compromise, others (like the 10mph lake speed limit) have resulted in full-scale battles. To set the scene on this Authority, it is perhaps appropriate to quote verbatim what the LDNPA have to say about themselves:

'It is patently clear that the quality of landscape and grandeur of scenery of the Lake District was the major factor in bringing

ABOVE: *The area has an abundance of birdlife, and the fells on a warm summer day are filled with the calls of skylark, lapwings, snipe and the common red grouse seen here at nest. If you are lucky, you might also catch a glimpse of the magnificent birds of prey, such as the golden eagles that live in these mountains.* SP

BELOW: *National Trust workers repairing the Westmorland slate roof of a vernacular farm building at Side Farm.* NT

about a system of statutory protection and recognition of this north western corner of England. The Lake District National Park was created under the provisions of the National Parks and Access to the Countryside Act 1949 and came into being on the 15th August 1951. The present National Park Authority was set up under the Environment Act 1995. Covering 880 square miles, the Lake District National Park is the largest, most spectacular and one of the most visited of Britain's 11 National Parks.'

The evolution of National Parks dates back to the classical poets - Wordsworth, Coleridge and Southey, and later Ruskin - all of whom devoted considerable energy to literary descriptions of the Lake District. Wordsworth, who lived in Grasmere, has been credited with originating the concept. He referred to the Lake District as a sort of national property in which every man has a right and interest who has an eye to perceive and a heart to enjoy.' [On page 71 we have given the Lake District Park Authority the opportunity to add a little more information about their activities today.]

The First Moves By Lakeland's Guardian

There can be no doubt that after the poets, it was the work of the vicar of Crosthwaite, Keswick (Canon Hardwicke Drummond Rawnsley) that inspired so many others to join together to protect this special area. Following Wordsworth's early efforts, it was Rawnsley who did so much, helping Miss Octavia Hill and Sir Robert Hunter to found the National Trust in 1895. It is therefore not hard to appreciate why Rawnsley justifiably became known as Lakeland's Guardian when he launched his crusade to protect it from harm and over-development. It was on Ullswater that the first big campaign began, for it was here that Rawnsley and Miss Hill launched the public appeal to 'save Gowbarrow Park for the nation' only 11 years after the National Trust was launched.

After the intervention of World War I, Rawnsley again drew public attention to the plight of the Lakes in a letter to the *Times*, in which he first raised the subject of a National Park or reserve for the area. The nation-wide debate that this sparked was still continuing when Rawnsley died in May 1920, but the call was getting louder.

Another campaigner on behalf of the Lake District was Rufus H. Mallinson, who wrote in a local newspaper condemning the new phenomenon of telegraph poles, which he said were disfiguring the landscape. He took various photographs for the press, and these clearly showed just how out of place the poles were at places like Kirkstone Pass and over Shap. Although this was a full three quarters of a century ago, even then the campaigners were alert to the preference of taking cables underground. The eyesores that Mr. Mallinson campaigned against in his article ironically have modern counterparts, and at various points around Cumbria the sight of modern wind-turbine generators provide the same source of annoyance to modern day country lovers.

The Lake District National Park

The National Park idea was discussed at a conference arranged by the Council for the Protection of Rural England at Manchester in October 1929. Styled as the 'National Conference for The Preservation of Lakeland' it attracted Sir Charles Trevelyan (the Minister of Education), Viscount Ullswater and many others of like mind, and was undoubtedly a landmark event for it attracted around 350 people. There was even a special session at Ambleside on the weekend of 12-13th October, but its timing was really rather unfortunate. Just eleven days later, the infamous Wall Street Crash took place and the great Depression was on its way. It was therefore to be another 22 years before the objectives of the Campaign for the Protection of Rural England were achieved!

The conference did however bring out some important issues, and a wide variety of views were expressed. In all 68 societies, ranging from local rambling clubs to the National Trust, made sure that calls for the Lakes' needs were going to be heeded. Representatives of local councils were also present, and the speeches included calls not to make Lakeland a 'rural Blackpool' but instead to make efforts to form a new National Park. One delegate suggested that a single motorcar would spoil the peace and loneliness of places such as Styhead Pass for hundreds of walkers. Another talked of an 'ostrich complex', where people appeared to be burying their heads in the sand. He pointed out that few realised the dangers Lakeland was facing from the new motor age, the environment of the petrol pump, the growth of modern civilisation, litter, bungalows and telegraph or electricity poles, and any number of other ills.

Amid suggestions that a Government inquiry into National Park status for the Lake District would be set up, the Minister came straight to the point by stating that drastic steps had to be taken. He then went on record saying, that in order to prevent the destruction of the Lakes, he fully backed the idea of founding a new Lake District National Park.

By the end of World War II, progress on the National Park proposals had come to a virtual halt, and much of the region was in a sorry state. Large areas of land around Ullswater had been taken over for military training (especially on Askham Common and around Lowther). Elsewhere anything but vital estate maintenance work had ceased as men went off to war. This led to a backlog of maintenance on gates, walls, fences, paths and buildings of the Lakes, and the woodlands suffered worst of all. While politicians argued about problems with public transport, coal, housing and so on, Lakeland (far removed from Westminster) was a very low priority. However, the atrocious hardships of the bad winter in 1947 finally made Government listen, due to the precarious state of the local economy. With the end of hostilities, the demand for holidays, day trips and leisure increased considerably, and as blazing hot

Maintaining both the natural and the built environment is an important part of the work of Lakeland's custodians.

ABOVE: *National Trust forester, Steve Dowson, clears away a dangerous tree at Yew Crag.* NT

BELOW: *Both natural and man-made pressures can affect the built environment, and historic walls and bridges suffer considerable damage. Here National Park workers rebuild a slate bridge in Long Sleddale.* LDNPA

Although there are many who would like to see the Lakes return to wilderness status, one can not escape the fact that the area has been heavily affected by the hand of man for centuries. Amongst his works have been some remarkably attractive buildings created from natural local materials. Such buildings need much care and careful development in order to fulfil a modern role, yet still retain their character.

ABOVE: *Hartsop Hall.* NT

BELOW: *Farm buildings alongside Sandwick Beck.* AE

summers were recorded in 1946 and 1947, the pressures on the Lakes resumed.

Yet, despite the apparent lack of action, pressure from people wanting the formation of National Parks had led the powers that be to begin to seriously consider the future. The mass trespass on Kinder Scout in the Peak District on 24th April 1932 had also brought forward the issues of access to the countryside and footpaths. So was born the Hobhouse Report of 1946, in which the provision of National Parks, designation of public rights of way and open access were recommended to Government.

The Act was passed in 1949, and in 1950 a delegation from the National Parks Commission visited the area. The following year the Commissioners presented their plans for the extent of the new Lake District National Park. The boundaries they set (which now enclose one third of the County of Cumbria) extended from Caldbeck in the north to Lindale in the south, from Ravenglass in the west to Shap in the east and have not changed since their designation.

New Lakeland Society Founded

In June 1934, the Friends of The Lake District were formed to preserve the region's charm, and events such as the felling of trees on the Askham side of Lowther Castle (to afford better views) showed that they were much needed. The chief aims of this new group, officially titled the Lake District National Reserve Association, were:

1. To keep the public informed of the policies, affecting the Lake District, in the 1931 report of the National Parks Committee, and particularly to press for a unified policy for the District as a whole;
2. To mobilise local and national opinion to ensure that planning authorities stuck to the guidelines contained in the Town and Country Planning Act of 1932, and;
3. Set up a fund that would be used by local authorities to provide assistance or compensation to farms and other valuable businesses in the District, which could be adversely affected by the new rules meant to protect the landscape.

The earliest challenges faced by the 'Friends' included the telegraph poles on Kirkstone Pass and elsewhere, and blocking the sale of places such as Buttermere, Crummock Water and Loweswater to private landowners. 'It would have been an awful thought', said Sir Charles Trevelyan at the Friends' first big meeting, 'that the loveliness of Buttermere might be changed to a shore dotted with red-roofed bungalows.'

He was talking of a lake several miles west of Ullswater, but the problem was the same all around the Lake District. The National Council of Ramblers' Federation (which effectively went on to become the Ramblers' Association) and several other groups who feared their rights of way would be badly affected by private landowners, all supported the foundation of the Friends. They were soon to prove their mettle and the first major success in the Ullswater district came in January 1948, when the entire 2,260-acre Glencoyne Park estate, together with its distinctive old farmhouse, was purchased and handed over to the National Trust.

Undoubtedly the single most important pressure facing the Lakes today is the private motor car. Try driving from Kendal to Ambleside on a bank holiday morning and see this for yourself. Once evidenced, even the most totally dependent car-user will agree that something has to be done to ease the pressure. Experiments in traffic management have been tried at a number of locations, but as yet we have not reached the total exclusion status like those enforced on Peak District roads in the Goyt Valley and the Upper Derwent Valley.

Back in 1973 an idea was muted in the local press about putting gates across the entrance to the Howtown road to deter tourists from using it after serious congestion problems led the police to close the road for a few hours on several occasions that summer. There was opposition to the concept and the 'gates' idea never went any further. Yet if visitors fail to ignore the obvious problems with this road, the decision to exclude traffic may occur to someone else. What is therefore urgently required, is a good alternative transport system to ensure that such vital protective measures are implemented with viable alternatives for those who want to visit these areas.

The world's first National Park - Yosemite, which includes the Sierra Nevada region of California, has grasped the nettle in a big way. There Park Authorities have got tough with car owners and have simply banned them from the area altogether and visitors now have to leave their cars outside the Park and use public transport throughout. Other parks in the USA are beginning to follow Yosemite's lead, and a call has gone out for the English National Parks to do the same.

However, as it stands at present public transport has a long way to go, but it could be sympathetically developed and the authorities are doing what they can to achieve this. As Local Agenda 21 initiatives begin to take effect, more sustainable forms of transport may become available. Given the correct incentives visitors may then feel more willing to leave their cars behind, and take to public travel for part, if not all, of their journey through the Lakes. After all this is what the lake steamers have been doing for decades now. More integrated transport, the re-opening of the Penrith to Keswick rail route (currently being muted) and secure car parking with bus or cycle links would undoubtedly do much to help.

Ullswater offers so many activities to a wide ranging audience. From yachting or diving in the lake; from strenuous rock climbs to family walks, and from gourmet meals to alfresco picnics.

TOP: *Yachts at their moorings by the Ullswater Yacht Club.* ML

CENTRE: *Descending into Boredale.* SE

BOTTOM: *Picnics on the summit of Place Fell in high summer.* SE

 THE NATIONAL TRUST

Hartsop Hall

Throughout this book we have made frequent reference to the National Trust and its work, for it is one of the biggest land-owners in the Ullswater area. Yet few visitors will appreciate exactly what work the Trust does, or the role it plays in providing facilities for visitors and balancing this with the needs of its tenant farmers. To provide a greater understanding the Trust have contributed the following overview of their work.

'Around 14,000 years ago the Lake District was in the grip of the last great Ice Age. As it receded it left bare and barren valleys that, in time, became green, lush and covered in a tangle of trees, scrub and swamp. Man arrived 5,000 years ago and began the long process of change that has left the valleys as we see them today.

When the National Trust bought its first property in the Ullswater valley in the early 1900s, it found what was possibly the high point of an 'almost' perfect rural community, in that nothing was under threat and nature had been 'tamed'. This was largely due to the fact that, due to the terrain and type of land holding, a balance had been developed and maintained.

The big threats came after World War II, as the government paid farmers to produce more and more livestock (cattle and sheep), whilst the Forestry Commission rented large tracts of land and filled them with plantations of quick-growing softwood trees. All of which was done in the hope of national self-sufficiency! More recently the very people that come to admire the stunning landscapes began to pose a threat in the form of damage to land, air and water.

Of course, the big question is what do we want to see in Ullswater in 100 years time? Land management is a long term project and planning is essential. There are people with the view that parts of the Lake District could revert to 'wilderness', others want to maintain the present pattern of land use. The problem that the National Trust faces in the future is getting the balance right between conservation, farmer and tourist, for the needs of each group affects the landscape in different ways.

Government policy has changed in the Lake District National Park, with the creation of Environmentally Sensitive Areas (ESA), where grant money goes to farmers to aid the conservation of the countryside. This is giving the Trust the opportunity to work with their farm tenants on whole farm plans, giving a greater opportunity to affect the landscape. Possible changes in the Common Agricultural Policy and farming subsidies in the next few years, could have a very strong effect on upland farming, and thus bring further problems or opportunities.

Whatever is decided, the National Trust sees the protection of the environment as a high priority, and its statement of environmental principle states that it must.

1. *Prevent avoidable damage caused by human impact on the environment.*

2. *Protect the National Trust's long-term interests from environmental damage.*

3. *Be an exemplar of good environmental practice.*

In Ullswater, as well as working with the farm tenants to conserve the landscape (and incurring high costs maintaining and repairing important vernacular buildings on the farms) the Trust is concentrating on the re-establishment of some semi-natural ancient woodlands. On the 4,500 acre Glencoyne Farm, the tenant farmer in co-operation with the National Trust has recently created a 166 acre (67 hectare) 'wilderness' on the site of an ancient wood. Let us hope that our descendants in 100 years time will enjoy it.'

If you want to know more about the trust, or wish to support its work by becoming a member, why not visit Aira Force where information can be obtained from the recruitment stand in the car park.

Alternatively, contact:

The National Trust, North West Office,
The Hollens, Grasmere, Ambleside, Cumbria LA22 9QZ

WHAT IS THE LAKE DISTRICT NATIONAL PARK?

The Lake District National Park is outstandingly beautiful, provides enjoyment to millions of people every year and is the home of over 40,000 residents. It possesses a unique combination of spectacular mountains and rugged fells penetrated by pastoral and wooded valleys, which are often mirrored in the numerous lakes and tarns. The character of the area is inseparable from the personalities, life-styles and traditions of the Lake District people. Each valley (including Ullswater) has its own individuality, a reflection of the rich and varied histories. It is this diversity, when found within such a relatively small area, that contributes so much to the attraction of the Lake District as a whole.

The National Park Authority recognises that it cannot safeguard the future of the Lake District on its own. The other local authorities, many agencies, business, voluntary bodies and individuals play their part and the National Park Authority works with them. You, the reader can also play a part, but few people understand what the work of the Authority entails. So, we present a few of the commonly asked questions, and the National Park Authority's answers:-

Why Do We Need National Parks?
To safeguard areas of particular outstanding natural beauty as national treasures, for the recreation and enjoyment of all!

Why Do We Need A Lake District National Park Authority?
Millions of visitors enjoy 11 national parks in England and Wales, creating a heavy burden of administration for local councils. The National Park Authority, funded by the tax payer through central government, provides an extra tier of local government responsible primarily for conservation and protection - independent of, but working with, other landowners!

Who Are The Lake District National Park Authority?
The Authority has 26 members. Seven are elected members of district councils, seven come from Cumbria County Council, five are from parish councils, and seven are appointed by the Secretary of State!

Who Works For The National Park Authority?
There are around 170 staff working in planning, park management, visitor services and administration. The LDNPA owns only 4% of the land in the Park. Its Head Office is in Kendal, and it has other offices and depots in the National Park. It also has eight tourist information centres, plus two in partnership with others, and operates the Lake District Visitor Centre at Brockhole!

What Do The National Park Authority Do?
* *We carry out planning functions otherwise undertaken by a county or district council ensuring that any development is appropriate both to the landscape and the needs of local people;*
* *We repair and improve footpaths over a total of 3,595kms of rights of way keeping them accessible;*
* *By giving grants and advice, we work to enhance town and countryside;*
* *We repair drystone walls, protect flower meadows, woodlands and lakeshore habitats, plant trees and restore hedgerows;*
* *We provide a full information service to visitors, educational opportunities, an events programme, and a wide range of publications to help raise awareness and an understanding of the National Park!*

For those who wish to know more about the life and work of the Lake District, the Brockhole Visitor Centre is highly recommended as a place to visit. A full programme of events and activities is available from any information centre.

ACKNOWLEDGMENTS

This book is the work of many hands, and to the following individuals a great debt of gratitude is offered:

Warren Allison and the people of Glenridding; Photographs credited GRC
Alistair Aynscough; news story research
Robert Berry; bus service research
Dr. Ian Bottomley; Geological Notes
Robin Brunsall, Mine History Notes
Ranald A. M Coyne; Ullswater Steamer Notes
Cumberland & Westmorland Herald; archive facilities
Cumbria County Council; Heritage Services
Cumbria County Council; Public Transport Notes
Dalemain Estates; Dalemain Notes
David Brown Group; Photograph credited DBT
Durham University; Mining Notes
English Heritage; Historic Building Notes and Photograph credited EH
Judith Derbyshire; National Trust Notes
Emma Dewhurst; National Park Notes
Professor Alan Earnshaw; Transport/Roman History Notes and Photographs credited AE
Larraine Earnshaw; Photographs credited LE
Sarah Earnshaw; Photographs credited SE
Dave Freeborn; Mountain Rescue Team Notes and Photgraphs credited DF
Christian Grammer; Ullswater Steamer Notes and Photographs credited CG
Glenridding Hotel; Photographs credited GH
Hutton In The Forest Estate; Hutton In The Forest Notes
Dr. Alan Johnson; Celtic History Notes
Ron Kenyon; Photographs credited RK
Michael Laycock; Photographs credited ML
Don Lord, Ullswater Community College
Adam M. Magnusson; Viking History Notes
John Melling, Glenridding Hotel;
Sam Murphey; Photographs credited SM
Patterdale Mountain Rescue Team; Photographs credited PMRT
Professor Stuart Payne; Local History & Archeology Notes
Penrith Agricultural Society; Agricultural Notes
Dr. Andrew Richards; Geological Notes
Ken Ratcliffe; National Trust Notes
The Lake District National Park Authority Photographs credited LDNPA
The National Trust, for their kind assistance and those Photographs credited NT
The Metreological Office; Weather Notes
Ullswater Transit & Navigation Co.; Ullswater Steamer Notes
Venture Publishing Ltd., Glossop; Photograph credited JS/VP
(and for permission to quote from their book *Cumberland Motor Services*)
Tony Wakefield; Photograph credited TW
Stephen White, Carlisle Library archive facilities
Windermere Steam Boat Museum